For my daughter Natasha, whose sunny nature,
quiet confidence and philosophical attitude are
great sources of inspiration.

....

Acknowledgements

Thanks to all the mums and dads who have shared their experiences within the book, the many organizations that offer support to parents and children, my family for their patience and support, and Victoria Roddam and the team at Hodder for giving me the opportunity to write this book.

Contents

Meet the author

As the mum of a bright and breezy 12-year-old, I've seen a lot of highs and lows in her confidence, influenced by all sorts of factors: friendships (new and broken); school work (struggles as well as successes); body development (and being nearly a year younger than some of her year group, you can imagine!) and more. I've also had the privilege of being stepmother to two, now grown-up children, so I have first-hand experience of the sorts of challenges that lie ahead in parenting.

I came to motherhood with a long professional background in the parenting press and, as such, news of my pregnancy was greeted with a whole lot of comments from friends and colleagues along the lines of 'Well at least you're well prepared, knowing so much already'. Even the midwife at my booking appointment wrote in thick black capitals across my notes: 'Parenting journalist', and seemed surprised when I asked her to treat me as she would any newly expectant first-time mum. I asked her how she'd felt when she was expecting her first baby, and she'd replied with honesty that all her midwifery knowledge flew out the window when it came to her own pregnancy and birth; suddenly she understood where I was coming from.

Raise A Confident Child has been written as a companion to lifelong parenting, starting from the very beginning, with hints on how confidence-building can start in pregnancy and infancy, right up to and beyond that heart-in-mouth moment when our fledglings are finally ready to leave home for the first time. It's packed with strategic advice on the importance of giving constructive feedback and when and how to deliver it; helping children form and manage relationships; supporting them through their schooldays; steering them through life's disappointments and traumas; tapping into their potential; surviving (and enjoying) their teen years; encouraging them towards greater independence; empowering them to take responsibility for their own lives and equipping them with the skills to face whatever the future may hold. The '10 things to remember' sections at the end of each chapter are designed to give you instant reminders of the key points for when you need advice fast, and the book is peppered with anecdotes and tips from real parents.

Please note that references throughout the book to 'middle school' describe the lower part of secondary school with students aged between 9 and 13. The term 'high school' is used to describe either all or part of secondary school with students aged between 11 and 16–18.

I hope you'll dip into the book for advice at each stage of each of your children's development, and I hope you find it thought-provoking and entertaining as well as useful.

Only got a minute?

There's one quality we can nurture in our children that's essential for happiness, success, building strong relationships and generally getting the most out of life: *confidence*. When you think about it, it's at the root of all other positive characteristics. The child who lacks confidence finds it harder to make friends, shies away from participating in the classroom, can be reluctant to try new experiences and often fears independence. Granted, there's a fine line between confidence and arrogance, and it's our input as parents that will, for the most part, influence which of these traits our children most often display.

Building confidence in children (and in adults, for that matter) is an important skill to learn. There's a world of difference, for instance, between simply punctuating conversations with 'Well done' or 'Clever girl' and delivering well-timed, germane praise. The main premise of confidence building is to make praise specific, and to accompany it with plenty of demonstrative love. Another key to confidence is to provide your growing family with an easy-to-understand framework of rules so they know where the boundaries for safe and acceptable behaviour lie. How can a child 'test the boundaries' if there are none in place? Far from cramping a child's creativity and independence, sensibly thought-out rules encourage exploration within safe limits and demonstrate our care and concern as parents.

Because each child is an individual, there's no single, failsafe prescription for building lasting confidence, but even when it seems as if the wheels are falling off your confidence-building wagon, don't despair. As long as you continue to deliver plenty of praise in a loving, proud and – importantly – specific way, as well as making any criticism constructive, you'll soon get back on track.

1

Why confidence matters

In this chapter you will learn:
- *what confidence means and when to start building it*
- *the importance of trust*
- *how confidence and independence are interdependent*
- *how your own experiences can impact on your child's confidence*

What is confidence?

Dictionaries variously give the definition of confidence as faith, assurance and certitude, and these are certainly among the qualities parents hope to instil in their children. But confidence isn't only *about* the self; it comes from *within* the self, and extends to the way in which we view other people and the world around us; it's about trust, security and respect; it's about counting on ourselves and others. You may have heard the terms 'emotional literacy', 'emotional quotient (EQ)' or 'emotional intelligence'. Each of these soundbites describes the ability to recognize and appropriately express our emotions – and this ability is a life skill that forms another vital part of self-confidence.

From childhood we need to feel confident that our parents and other adults are trustworthy, reliable and constantly there for us; we need to place our confidence in teachers and child carers. We can only respect others if we feel confident about their motives towards us and their own integrity and we can't make progress without confidence in our own abilities and the support of other people. So 'confidence' is a big word encompassing a large number of ideals. It's also a vital tool for healthy, happy growth and fulfilment, and one which – when built from an early age – can help our children to achieve their potential, and to celebrate that achievement.

This chapter gives an overview of the importance of confidence and a taster of some of the key ways we can encourage it in our children at each stage of development. There are lots more details on each age and stage later in the book.

Where do we start?

Confidence-building can start before a child is even born: research studies have proven that a newborn baby reacts and responds to the voices of their mother and other adults who have been around regularly during pregnancy, and that they find these familiar voices both soothing and reassuring. From birth, babies trust their caregivers instinctively: they take comfort from being picked up; they prefer people whose voices they are familiar with over strangers; they cry and expect the appropriate response. It's never too soon to build on this instinctive confidence: by learning to recognize your baby's needs and respond to them, you're reinforcing the idea that you are caring, reliable and trustworthy.

> *I wasn't at all sure I'd be a good enough mother, but when Jamie was born and she gazed straight into my eyes in recognition when I spoke to her, I knew we'd be all right.*

Hayley, mum to Jamie, three months

Insight
Remember, confidence building can start in the womb. So:

- ▶ find times to focus on your baby when they are at their most active
- ▶ talk in soothing tones to your baby
- ▶ sing to your baby
- ▶ get your partner involved with chatting to your baby
- ▶ stroke your bump, especially during your baby's wakeful times.

INFANCY

In the early weeks of life, a newborn's confidence comes from having their needs recognized and met promptly; routines can be brought in later (from around six weeks or so) but before then, lay the groundwork for their continuing trust in you by responding to them immediately when they need food, comfort, security or warmth. You can't spoil a baby: it takes many months before an infant even begins to learn how to manipulate people to their own advantage, and by then you'll have had a chance to explore the different settling routines and to find one that suits you and your baby. Shower them with kisses and cuddles and soothe them by holding them close to you, skin on skin. Get your partner and any other regular carers to do the same. Your baby will gain confidence from the knowledge that you're there for them when they need you.

> *My mum-in-law was all for me leaving Sam to cry, even when he was hungry. She said babies only needed feeding every four hours and had to learn to settle themselves. I went along with her for the first two days and it was sheer hell. Once I'd decided to feed on demand and pick Sam up to settle him when he cried, life became instantly more bearable as he learned that I would respond to him straight away.*
>
> Jenni, mum to Sam, six weeks

Insight

A baby sling allows you to carry and soothe your baby, leaving your hands free. Lots of parents find this an invaluable aid in the early days when newborns are relatively lightweight, and your baby will love the close contact, which will make them feel safe as well as cosy.

TODDLERHOOD

There are so many opportunities for building or knocking your toddler's confidence that it can seem like treading through a minefield, but key pointers for building confidence at this stage are allowing independence and creating opportunities for socializing, as well as making regular, special one-to-one times for them, especially if you have a younger baby as well. Issues with difficult behaviour usually arise in toddlerhood, and it's easy to label children unthinkingly in ways that will only perpetuate the behaviour. To avoid this, criticize the behaviour, not the child, so instead of saying 'You horrible boy, hitting your sister!' try 'We all know that hitting is nasty' instead.

A child who has a clear understanding of their own wants and dislikes but doesn't have the language to convey them will expect you to mind-read – and may fall into fits of furious frustration if you don't comprehend what they are trying to tell you. But there's a fine line between understanding and over-indulgence here and this is explored in detail later. It's all about keeping the communication between the two of you as clear and direct as possible at this stage, and everything you can do to make that easier is well worth trying.

> *I taught my daughter, Sienna, to 'sign' from babyhood and it paid dividends when she was a toddler. Although there were still some protests over what I would or wouldn't let her do, we didn't have any of the screaming tantrums that come from being unable to say what you mean as she could use the sign language we'd devised between us.*

Andrea, mum to Sienna, two and a half

Insight

Toddler behaviour is always at its worst when your child is tired, bored or hungry. Try to avoid taking them to the supermarket, or anywhere equally tedious to a toddler, when they really need to chill out, eat or sleep. And when you do venture out together, keep a healthy snack, a drink and an amusing toy to hand.

THE OLDER CHILD

Once your child is approaching school age and realizes that they will have to become a bit more grown up and spend lots of time away from you, you're very likely to see their confidence diminishing and old insecurities surfacing once more. They may start to become clingy; they may be more prone to tantrums or tears than normal; they may be reluctant to even discuss going to school – in fact, they might find it very hard to articulate their anxieties or even understand where they're coming from. You may find that they're really reluctant to start school if they have a younger sibling at home, protesting that it's not fair that the baby can stay home with you and they can't. This is perfectly understandable, but you can help them to feel better about it all by taking steps to rebuild their confidence. Remind them of all the skills they already have that will stand them in good stead for school. These could include self-dressing and feeding; holding a pencil; colouring in; playing games and sports and being good at puzzles. Point out that all their friends will be starting school, too, and that their little brother or sister will be looking up to them as the big kid when the time comes for them to start school. Have some special treats set aside for them at the end of their school day, too, like a favourite DVD to watch together, a trip to the park on the way home or a visit to their grandma, who'll be very keen to hear all about their day. This will give them the confidence that you understand their worries and care enough to make them feel better. Be at the ready with plenty of hugs and kisses; this is a rule that's going to apply throughout this book because it applies throughout their childhood and way beyond! There's nothing more likely to build confidence and self-assurance than physical expressions of love, along with praise and encouragement. Help them to try to identify and articulate their emotions. Ask questions that describe how they might be feeling, such as: 'Does the thought of starting school make you feel excited or scared – or a bit of both?', 'Do you feel worried about a particular thing?' or 'How do you think you'll manage with [something they usually need help with]?' Reassure them about likely anxieties by saying things like: 'I think your teacher is going to really like you in her class' and 'Won't it be exciting to have some new friends to play with?' and 'It's a big step going to big school, I remember, but soon you'll feel as if you really belong.' Later in the book we'll see how allowing your child to revert to babyish behaviour for a while will, rather than being a retrograde step, actually help build their confidence and set them back on track.

Some children seem to relish the run-up to starting school and show a lot of bravado as the day draws closer. If this is your child, it'll be a relief to you that they're so looking forward to being a big child at school – but, although they may make the transition perfectly smoothly, do be prepared for a slight fall-back on their enthusiasm once they realize that school is a long-term thing, or if it's actually a bit more daunting than they were expecting. Don't forget that, apart from any induction meetings or school socials they've attended and the home visit their teacher may have made in the run-up to joining, they won't have a very clear idea of what school life will actually be like.

My mum used to tell me not to be such a baby when I wanted my old cot blanket after school some days. I didn't realize at the time but I can see now that it made me feel very insecure when she was actually trying to make me more independent. Harry still takes his favourite teddy everywhere he goes except school – and that's only in case he loses it. Luckily his school allows for a small, pocket-sized toy to be brought in, so he's got a special little school teddy that he takes with him to remind him of home.

Jason, dad to Harry, six, and Megan, four

Insight

If your child finds it hard to articulate their insecurities, encourage them to draw. You can often glean a lot about a child's emotional state from their drawings, which can open up possibilities for conversations they may otherwise find difficult.

TWEENIES

As your child teeters on the brink of becoming a teenager and makes the transition from middle school to high school, there's another whole set of issues lurking in the wings to threaten their confidence. From pre-pubescent spots to slow growth, awkwardness about body image and peer pressure to 'following the crowd', they'll be faced with one apparent crisis after another. This is not the time to take a back seat and let them sort it out for themselves, whatever the message they appear to be sending you. You will have to tread gently, yes, but this is the age when your child will need the reassurance that you're always there for them, even if they find it impossible to express their appreciation or even acknowledge your existence! You'll also probably have to fight your instincts if, for example, your child starts wanting to experiment with things that may seem inappropriate for their age. Don't forget that each successive generation of kids wants to try things younger than the one before – and as long as it's fairly innocent and not harmful in any way, your best bet is probably to go along with it. But don't be duped, either, into believing your child's protestations that 'everyone else is doing it!' If in doubt, check with some of their friends' parents. It's all tricky stuff – and you'll find more about it in a later chapter.

> *At first I was a bit horrified when my ten-year-old daughter wanted to wear make-up every weekend, but I calmed down, helped her choose some subtle shades, showed her how to apply them without looking slutty and then waited for the novelty to wear off. It only took about three weeks, and it was her own choice. Bingo!*

Helena, mum to Danielle, ten

Insight

Don't dismiss your child's insecurities by saying 'Of course you're not fat, don't be so silly!' or 'Everyone gets spots, so what?' Acknowledge what's troubling them, and try to make sense of it for them, for example, explain that some children (particularly girls) become a bit plumper as their rate of growth in height mismatches their growth in body fat. And don't forget those all-important hugs if they're welcome!

TEENAGE ANGST

Letting go is just about the hardest part of being a parent, and although your teenager isn't ready for full independence and will undoubtedly need a steer from you from time to time, the greatest confidence to be built here is in their own judgement and abilities. This is why it's important not to criticize their choice of friends/ clothes/music/language, and to give them some freedom to explore their likes and dislikes. They'll probably want to be just the same as their mates, getting into whatever the crowd likes. They might be a trend-setter or very much an individual – and good luck to them if they are, because it's also the measure of a pretty confident kid. So listen when they want to talk; sit on the sidelines a bit; give them some privacy; offer advice when appropriate; forgive, bail out, reprimand, reason. But don't criticize. And do discourage any younger siblings from making fun of them. Explain that this is a difficult time for their big brother and that they'll expect some understanding when they reach their age too.

> *Jay was mixing with a crowd I didn't really approve of for a while, but I encouraged him to bring them round to our house after school instead of hanging out on the streets, and they didn't seem to do any damage. I don't think he'd have wanted to bring them home if we'd been there too, but I think he appreciated being given the responsibility, and he respected us for it. He did move on from this group once he'd made his GCSE choices and found himself in different classes, but I think if we'd made a big deal about not liking them he might have dug his heels in.*
>
> Patty, mum to Jay, 15, and Daniel, 11

Insight

You're not necessarily expected to comment on your teen's appearance, so avoid doing so unless your opinion is asked for. Nothing will sound worse to some teenagers than 'You look nice, love,' with the possible exception of 'Cool, dude. Where can I get one of those?' (And while we're on the subject, nothing is more likely to irritate your teen than you trying to get 'down with the kids'. Don't even go there.)

YOUNG ADULT

It's tempting to think that once a child reaches the age of 18 or so, they're all sorted and ready to take their place in the adult world. In fact, it's not unusual for children to continue to feel like children well into their early 20s, however much bravado is flying around.

With adulthood comes the burden of real responsibility, and which of us wouldn't hand that back if given the opportunity! Your relationship may feel (with luck) as though it's moving more towards friendship than parent/child, but there are reasons why it's important to keep that boundary to a degree: this allows your child to fall back into younger behaviour without imagining they'll lose your respect; it also allows you to maintain some authority while still enjoying your 'child'. Later in the book you'll find tips on continuing to boost your child's confidence into adulthood. (This job, by the way, will never be at an end and goes hand-in-hand with unconditional love as one of the most precious gifts a parent can endow.)

> *I remember leaving home for the first time and my parents saying: 'You'll never manage; you'll be home in no time.' It wasn't very empowering, and when I got into credit card debt I didn't feel I could turn to them in case they said 'We told you so.' I had to borrow from my boyfriend's family, which was humiliating and meant I ended up staying in the relationship for far longer than was really healthy. I'll really try not to make that mistake with my two.*

Ellen, mum to Caterina, 20, and Eric, 17

Insight

Your role now is hopefully more supporter than rescuer (at least most of the time!), but it's a good idea to keep a small reserve of cash somewhere for the common financial disasters/crises that can occur as young adults strive to find their feet. Just don't tell them about it...

Trust, belief and confidence

How often do we refer to pieces of information we entrust to others as 'confidences'? This homophone is no coincidence: taking someone into our confidence implies that we trust them and feel confident of their integrity. Trusting your child will help to build feelings of self-esteem, as well as giving them the opportunity to contribute their own opinions and advice in any family discussion. (This isn't the same as you acting on their opinions or advice, by the way – although you may find they have better ideas than you do in some situations.) By the same token, listening to your child's own confidences – should you be privileged enough to be told – and keeping them to yourself unless it's absolutely unavoidable to do otherwise, will engender feelings of mutual trust and closeness. It will also encourage your child to be open, honest and frank with you, especially if you're open-minded.

HOW THEY LINK TOGETHER

Belief is also closely linked with confidence. If you can build up a culture of belief in your home, where it's assumed that everyone – your child included – habitually tells the truth, you'll be in a good position to believe whatever your child tells you, and this will boost their self-confidence. It's important, too, to make sure you balance this with the need for reasonable atonement when the truth is actually a confession. Don't rush in with a harsh punishment unless the confession is a grave one. First off, let your child know you appreciate their honesty; then discuss the reasons for the behaviour; empathize as far as possible; talk about the consequences of their actions and allow them to suggest ways of putting things right. Help them out on this last point only if they can't see how to go forward – and do issue a penalty where appropriate. You can even do this sympathetically and temperately by saying something along the lines of: 'Of course, we both know we can't just let the matter drop here. Sorry, but it means you'll have to forfeit an evening/week/month of instant messaging [or some other penalty that will have sufficient impact to act as a good deterrent] but hopefully that'll be the end of it.'

My daughter came home from school aged four, clutching a handful of 'treasure', which turned out to be a very appealing-looking collection of beads, buttons and sequins. When I asked her where she'd got it from she said she'd taken it from the craft box, and admitted that she'd just put a few of the nicest things in her pocket without asking. I gently pointed out that as she hadn't had permission this was a kind of stealing, and she was mortified. We agreed that she would tell the teacher she'd thought it would be OK to take some stuff, but offer to put it back. I didn't punish her, as she had misunderstood. However, a year or so later she came home from the school Christmas fair very tearful about having 'taken' a broken toy from the bric-a-brac stall for a dare. She knew what she'd done was wrong, even though the toy was broken, and immediately went to her piggy bank to find some money to give her teacher in payment the following day. Our compassion on the previous occasion had paid off, and although she did get a telling off for taking the toy, she also got some praise for owning up and putting things right on her own.

Helen, mum to Serena, seven

Insight

If your child chooses to confide in you about something you may find shocking or a bit eye-popping, try not to show your surprise. If your child detects any embarrassment or reticence on your part they'll probably decide to keep their thoughts to themselves next time, and a valuable bond will be broken. Act cool, even if you don't feel it.

Giving your child a voice

It's very easy to be a bit dismissive about our children's ideas and opinions – and it's fair to say that sharp-minded kids can be very good at putting 'spin' on their side of a discussion as a way of buying you in to their way of thinking! But, cynicism aside, they can also have a lateral way of looking at things that can actually spark off ideas that might not otherwise have occurred to you.

Allowing your child a voice – asking their opinion, listening to their views, valuing their input and including them in family conversations – will all boost their self-esteem and give them a sense of the value of their place within the family. And it doesn't have to stop at family discussions. Instigating conversation with them, aside from what they want in their sandwiches and how they got on at school, will also help to nurture independent thinking – which is brilliant for building confidence.

YOUR TODDLER

OK, so your toddler may not have dazzling insights into such thorny problems as where to holiday on a shoestring budget or how best to earn extra pocket money, but you can still encourage them to come up with their own ideas about everyday things. Try sitting and watching their favourite television programme and asking their opinion about it afterwards. You could ask which are their favourite characters and why, what they think might happen in the next episode, how many words/songs/actions they can remember and so on.

It's tempting to fill in missing words for your child when they're struggling to express themselves or when you're in a hurry and want them to get to the point, but it's well worth trying to bear with them whenever you can; they're probably mentally rummaging through their vocabulary when they pause before answering a question or when they get stuck telling you about their morning at nursery. If they become distressed or cross with themselves, by all means fill in some words for them, but if they're quite happily thinking, let them take their time to come up with the words they're searching for. If you do have to fill in, try to encourage your child to expand on whatever they were trying to say, to make them feel they've communicated effectively after all.

> *When Harry was a toddler, I used to set aside half an hour before lunch and after his morning nap for enjoying a book or DVD together. I'd put the answerphone on and switch my mobile to mute. Friends and family were also aware of our routine. The best part was talking about the story or film afterwards. I swear Harry's vocabulary began to really take off as a result, and he has lots of opinions and imaginative ideas now.*
>
> Sarah, mum to Harry, four

YOUR OLDER CHILD

In conversations with your school-age child, use a technique called 'reflecting': repeat back the information they have just shared with you before moving the conversation on. ('I see. Your teacher thinks you're great at science but you could do with some more help with maths. Well, it's helpful to know that, isn't it?') And do pause for long enough for your child to reply rather than rattling on by yourself, holding both sides of the conversation without their input!

Reflecting is particularly important when your child is sharing their feelings with you, so make a real effort to say things back to them to show you've heard and understood. For instance, say: 'So when your friend left you out of the football game, it made you feel sad and angry; yes, I can understand why you'd feel like that.' You can also build on this by encouraging your child to find solutions to problems: 'What will you do next time he leaves you out, do you think?' They may well come up with something not very constructive ('I'll smash his face in!') but with a little gentle steering they'll probably find their own answers, and this will make them feel empowered, mature and confident. (Because it's key to boosting your child's self-esteem, you'll be reminded about the reflecting technique often throughout the book.)

Talking to Anna about conflicts at school, we try to focus on how each person involved in an incident might be feeling, from the aggressor to the victim and both children's friends and classmates. It's given Anna a sense of empathy, and she's known as the class peacemaker now, which is lovely. I'm so glad she has the confidence to know what to say to each party.

Michelle, mum to Anna, eight

YOUR TWEENIE

You'll probably find that your tweenie is unsure about their own stance on things, veering from one set of opinions to another and swinging between wanting to be regarded as grown up and needing to be babied again. It's a challenging time (and there's still the teenage years to come!) but there are ways of bringing the confidence out at this in-between stage.

Try to avoid challenging their views where you can, although it's fine to acknowledge that they've changed. So instead of saying: 'You don't seem to know *who* you're friends with these days,' try saying 'That's a name I haven't heard before,' and let your child take it from there.

Tweenies famously tend to adopt the behaviour, look and attitude of teenagers, and this is fine as long as it doesn't go too far; allowing your tweenie to project forward to the next age stage is not so much different from when, as a toddler, they tried to run before they could walk. The time to step in is if the behaviour becomes totally age inappropriate, but in the meantime try to cut them a little slack where you feel that there's no real argument not to do so. So you might agree to your child joining a safe networking social website (with the appropriate privacy settings in place), but not permit them to visit unregulated online chat rooms; you might decide it's fine for them to go to the movies with their friends, but draw the line at them hanging out in the shopping mall all afternoon afterwards; you may award them a little more pocket money than in recent years, but block the idea that they can borrow your bank card to withdraw cash for themselves. Granting these small freedoms will help to build a bond of trust between you; it will give them a chance to show that they can behave responsibly, and therefore earn more freedoms as they grow up. On the other hand, withholding some privileges for now will maintain the boundaries that actually help to make them feel safe – so everyone's happy (or that's the theory!).

I was unsure about letting Adam have a social networking page, but when he had a problem with his mobile phone that meant he would have to stop using it for a month, I finally caved in because of the free chat facility. However, I made the condition that I would have to be one of his friends so I could keep some kind of tabs on his online activity. He's cool with that after some initial wrangling, and appreciates the fact that he's allowed the page at all. I'm not nosing over his shoulder at all times, but the knowledge that I can check his page after he's gone to bed does seem to keep him from posting or responding to anything slightly inappropriate, and the freedom he gets from chatting online has given him a certain amount of important 'cred' among his peers.

Mick, dad to Adam, 11

YOUR TEEN

As a teenager, your child will be used to having to be responsible for themselves in all sorts of situations: completing their homework; taking the correct stuff to school each day; organizing their own social life (up to a point!). You can increase their feelings of self-esteem by gradually giving them more small freedoms to endorse the fact that you trust them to act responsibly. So, for instance, look into getting them a bank account with a cash card so that they can have a little financial independence (but do some research first as there are a lot of accounts to choose from). Get them used to travelling on public transport if they aren't doing so already – an Oyster card is a good idea if you live in London or Greater London. Keep a system of penalties in place for if your teenager abuses your trust, and make it clear that they'll need to earn it back. Respect is a two-way thing, based on mutual trust.

If you do need to issue a penalty, try not to make it long and drawn-out; a fortnight's grounding will effectively enable you to keep tabs on your child, but a shorter, sharper punishment such as banning social use of the computer for a couple of days, means less impact on the rest of the family. Constructive penalties mean lessons can be learned too; so if your child has overspent, for instance, get them to spend the time they're missing on the PC drawing up a budgeting sheet, then encourage them to fill it in until they can better manage their cash. They may seem to hate you for it, but it'll actually reinforce the idea that you care about them and the way they're turning out.

Listening is as important during teenage years as at other times in childhood, and by now your child will probably have their own opinions on some important issues. (OK, they might be someone else's opinions that they've picked up because they admire that particular individual, but at least it shows they're interested in debate, so encourage them to talk about why they hold a particular view.) Try asking their opinion on relevant news stories too: if, for instance, one of the members of their favourite band hits the headlines, have a discussion about the story. This will also give you a gauge of where they're at emotionally, intellectually and socially.

> *I've found that making Eloise accountable for money has really boosted her confidence. As soon as she joined high school, for instance, she switched from wanting packed lunches to having school dinners, as her friends were doing the same and she was impressed by the various meals and snacks on offer in the canteen. Once she got into Year 8 we agreed that I would open a school catering account for her, which means putting a certain amount of credit in place and letting her use a swipe card to make purchases. After a couple of weeks of going a bit crazy with buying snacks – and a couple of occasions of having to ask her to pay up for them – she's acting very responsibly, making sensible food choices and managing the money well.*

Geri, mum to Eloise, 13

YOUNG ADULT

By now, your child must be encouraged to take responsibility for how their life is running: if the car breaks down, they should know who to call and how to organize themselves; if they're employed, they should be able to plan a route to work with some alternatives, all of which will get them there punctually; if they're not around at mealtimes, they should be able to sort themselves out something to eat. They'll probably still need an occasional steer when it comes to dealing with relationships of all sorts – with their employer, mates, boy- or girlfriend and colleagues. You can build up their confidence by talking to them frequently, listening and reflecting. If you sense something is on their mind, probe gently and see if they'll open up (and accept that they may not). If they have a particular worry, role-playing a solution can help as it did when they were a much younger child. If, for example, they need to confront their boss about something, role-play the meeting beforehand so they'll feel well equipped to answer any awkward questions and present their case without losing their cool.

Be prepared for some budgeting disasters too. If your child has recently left university, for instance, they may have a student debt to juggle with their other spending, so don't be too harsh on them. Or if they've gone straight from school to work – or being unemployed – they may also struggle. Help them to budget by showing them how you handle your own finances (if indeed you are a good role model!), and support them in any way you can. If you're lending them money, though, keep a tally of how much you've given them and when, plus details of any repayments they make to you. Set a deadline by which you'd like the money repaid too. They're going to have to deal with paying rent or a mortgage on time each month before long, so this is excellent training.

Above all, don't expect too much. Just because they've reached adulthood, it doesn't mean they don't feel out of their depth at times, and that can be quite confidence-lowering. Allow them to be a little childlike again if that's what they want. As long as they're moving in the right direction towards independence generally, there's no harm in letting them retreat into the safety of being a bit dependent from time to time. They probably won't feel comfortable showing anyone else their vulnerable side, after all.

We'd been amazed with how well Rory had adapted to finding a job and moving into rented accommodation after he came home from university. But one weekend, when we'd invited him for lunch, he admitted that it was all just too much to juggle and he'd come a bit unstuck. We gave him a hand with working out his budget and loan repayments, and reassured him that we would always be on hand to help if the going got tough. We offered to lend him a little cash to help him through the sticky patch, but just knowing we were on his side seemed enough to get him back on his feet. As it turned out, there was no real need for him to panic – he just wanted to be sure he had our backing. I think he'd been half expecting us to demand that he came home until his loan was repaid, but we have confidence that he'll manage OK.

Diana, mum to Rory, 22

Insight

Listening to our children is so important for confidence building, as it shows them that we value what they're saying to us – and the more we communicate effectively, the more they're likely to share information. Proper listening is, of course, quite different from half taking in what someone is telling us, so practise reflecting, described earlier in the chapter, where you frequently repeat back what you've been told to show you've heard and understood.

Encouraging independence

Independence goes hand-in-hand with confidence-building; you can't really expect one without the other. Being independent means having the self-belief to do things for yourself that others have previously done for you and it can be encouraged at every age and stage, from babyhood to adulthood.

▶ **Baby** When you hand your baby a weaning spoon and let them do their worst with their bowl of purée, you're showing them that you trust them to have a go at feeding themselves. When you prop them up with cushions and place some toys within their reach, you're giving them the confidence to make their own choices about what to play with next.

▶ **Toddler** When you put out a couple of outfits for your toddler and let them choose, you're telling them that you think they'll make a good job of trying to dress themselves. When you give them a wooden spoon and encourage them to stir a bowl of cake mix, you're showing them that you value their help and believe in their ability. (Just make sure you're both wearing aprons!)

▶ **Older child** When you listen to your older child reading, and you praise them and encourage them to sound out words rather than just telling them how to say them, you're encouraging them to think for themselves and instilling a sense of pride in their achievements. When you support them as they take their first swimming strokes, you're reinforcing the idea that they can handle themselves in the water and be confident in their ability.

▶ **Tweenie** When you invite your tweenie to go to the local shops and buy their own tea, you're not only proving that you trust them to look after themselves and interact with others in public, you're also entrusting them with your money and showing them that you believe they'll bring the right change back. When you allow them to make their own choices (within reason) when you shop for clothes, you're allowing them the freedom to express their own personality and style (at least at weekends!).

▶ **Teen** When you give your teenager their own house key, you're proving that you trust them to come and go responsibly, and to look after the house appropriately when you're not there. By encouraging them to bring friends back or go out with them, you're endorsing their choice of mates and letting them know that you believe they can act in a mature way.

▶ **Young adult** When you ask your young adult for opinions on family matters, you're showing that you think their thought processes and views are as valuable as your own. When you allow them to borrow the family car, you're giving them credit for driving responsibly and looking after your vehicle.

Not only will all these kinds of encouragement tell your child that you have confidence in them and their abilities and choices, they'll also build feelings of self-esteem, which are crucial for their happiness and success, both short and long term.

How your own experiences can impact on your child's confidence

Some of the ways in which you interact with your child will be founded on how you were treated as a child yourself. We can't help some of the attitudes towards our achievements (or lack of them) becoming entrenched in our own personalities – but with a little self-awareness, we can try to prevent them getting handed down the line. Your parents may have been either strongly supportive or hypercritical of your efforts during your formative years, or maybe they had a more balanced approach, were largely passive or were just rather uninvolved.

Whatever your own parents' approach, a good starting point is for you to sit down and list the positives and negatives of your experiences growing up with them. For instance, if a particular incident sticks in your mind (perhaps you still bristle with pride when you recall something your dad said to you following an achievement; or maybe you can still remember the hurt you felt when your mum inadvertently criticized your dress sense), write it all down and resolve to use the good and discard the bad when parenting your own children. It can be hard to stick to your guns, especially as you'll probably have absorbed these attitudes from your own childhood and may have a tendency to replicate them, but keep the list somewhere private where you can refer to it regularly until you know you can rely on yourself to make the best judgements as you go along. (Make sure you forgive yourself any hiccups along the way, though; these are perfectly natural and understandable while you retrain yourself.) The ultimate aim is to break any negative cycles of criticism and reproduce cycles of praise and confidence-building.

There's another way your experiences can be helpful to your child, too – as evidence that you were once their age and made many mistakes of your own. See if you can recall specific examples of misjudgements you made in your youth, or hare-brained schemes that came to nothing. Tell them how it felt at the time to have failed, how you moved on from the experience and how it benefited you in the end. It's a great way of showing them that there's usually value in all life's experiences, even the less positive ones.

CASE STUDY

Why my youngest is more confident than his older siblings

When Frankie was born I had such high expectations, both of myself as a mother and of him as a potential achiever, that the pressure I put us both under was almost unbearable. I think it stemmed from my parents always expecting great things from me and my sister. I loved Frankie like mad – unconditionally, or so I thought – but it turned out that every time he was outdone by one of his peers, I somehow managed to show my disappointment. Likewise, I'd beat myself up if I didn't produce the perfect meal every night (more so if Frankie didn't seem to enjoy his food), or if I didn't keep the house spick and span at all times, and if I was anything but calm and collected each evening when my partner, Mark, came home.

Things changed considerably when we had Amy. By then, Frankie was four and quite a reticent child, worried about taking risks and wary of contributing anything in the school classroom for fear of getting something wrong. I knew I'd been misguided and had set him up for fall after fall from the time he was able to understand what I wanted from him. I felt terribly guilty, but I couldn't go back and make it right. With Amy to look after as well, lots of my ridiculously high standards had to fall by the wayside: the house was rather more lived in than it had previously been; the washing was always spilling out of the laundry bin and washing machine (and still is!). I resorted more and more to convenience foods and I was all but ready for bed by 8pm! As a result, though, I hardly put myself or Amy under any pressure to achieve and perform, and I could see that she was much more carefree than Frankie had been at her age.

We had Tom more by accident than design, I have to admit. I was barely coping with the demands of two children, and by the time he was born, Frankie was seven and Amy was three. Everything went completely haywire with my quest for perfect motherhood, and the only approach open to me was to let the kids more or less get on with life, except for the bits they really needed help with.

A few years on and Tom has recently started school. He's outgoing, confident and adventurous, and completely oblivious to the fact that I have any expectations of him, either academically or in terms of developmental milestones. He's by far the happiest of the three children and is gregarious and well-loved by his peers. Amy is pretty confident too, although to a lesser degree than Tom, but that may be to do with the fact that more is expected of her at school now as well. But as for Frankie, he's still not willing to take risks and will turn to Mark for help with anything he thinks might otherwise disappoint me. I do feel terribly guilty, and am trying now to limit the damage by heaping praise on him at every opportunity and trying not to expect too much of him. I'd certainly advocate a more relaxed approach to parenthood, and would do things differently if I were able to turn the clock back. The atmosphere in the family home is definitely much happier now.

Jayne is mum to Frankie, 11, Amy, seven and Tom, four

10 THINGS TO REMEMBER

1 Confidence begins before birth, so stroke your bump and talk and sing to your baby in pregnancy.

2 You can't spoil a young baby, so give them lots of cuddles and all the reassurance they need.

3 Avoid creating situations where your child will be likely to need telling off: try not to take them out shopping or visiting when they're tired, hungry or under the weather.

4 When they misbehave, criticize the behaviour, not them; labelling them is likely to reinforce the bad behaviour.

5 It's all right to let your older child regress to more baby-like behaviour as they gain independence – it's quite normal and will make them feel safe.

6 Don't take rebuffs from your tweenie seriously; they're likely to need your support more than ever, even if they seem to want the opposite.

7 Support your teenager's sense of individuality as far as possible – it will help them build a strong sense of identity.

8 If they prefer to follow the crowd, don't be too critical; they may gain more confidence from fitting in than striking out.

9 Gradually increase the amount of responsibility you give your older teenager – but make clear that it's dependent on them showing that they're equal to it.

10 It's lovely when young adults become more like friends to their parents, but it's vital you keep the adult–child boundary in place to some degree in order for your child to feel they have someone to fall back on.

The power of praise

In this chapter you will learn:
- *how to praise effectively*
- *how praise can have a negative impact*
- *ways children seek approval*
- *how to handle 'over-confidence'.*

The role of praise

You're going to read the word 'praise' often throughout this book. This is because it's the very key to confidence, and a lack of praise leads to feelings of low self-esteem and even, in some cases, worthlessness. Children, however, are highly proficient at distinguishing insincerity and false praise from the genuine article, so do resist the urge to go over the top. One way of ensuring the praise you offer is accepted without question is to refer specifically to whatever it is you're praising. So instead of saying: 'Well done, my precious princess,' it might be more helpful (and less saccharine) to say 'I love the way you've made the sky pink in your picture – how imaginative!' But over-praising – that is, praising for every behaviour or action, even those which are expected or should bring their own reward, like playing nicely or reading a book, can lead to a child lacking any motivation without praise. Better in these circumstances to say 'I'm glad you're enjoying that book,' or 'Isn't it fun when you play well together?' which gives a positive message at the same time as saying that this is what's expected and it isn't exceptional.

Praise not only helps build confidence, it's also a very useful tool in encouraging good behaviour, as children are motivated (at least at the outset) by getting approval. So if you can do your best to ignore any unimportant misdemeanours in your child, but consistently give praise for positive behaviour, you'll not only notice them puffing up with pride before your very eyes, you should also see more of the good stuff and less of the bad. It's very easy to carp on about undesirable behaviour and ignore the positives, but psychologists believe that praise should outweigh criticism by about five times to one, so try giving positive feedback for little things that might usually go by without comment: 'Well done getting dressed when I asked you to'; 'Thanks for taking your plate out to the kitchen'; 'Haven't you brushed your hair nicely!' and so on.

> *I used to tell Kyle off quite a lot when he was two, but then my health visitor advised me to try and give him more praise for when he was good than criticism for when he wasn't. Within a week his behaviour was loads better and I felt a whole lot less stressed!*

Jenna, mum to Kyle, three

Insight

Praise is always so much more effective when it's specific. Think about your own life: would you rather, for example, your employer patted you on the back and said 'Good job!' when you completed a task ahead of target, or would you prefer to hear 'Thanks to your speed and efficiency with that last job we're well ahead of the game'? The same thinking applies to your child and their individual efforts.

Why praising effort is more important than praising intelligence

Some children are innately more intelligent than others, and although IQ can be improved upon, in some cases there are limits. Effort, on the other hand, has a much wider scope for improvement, and can be encouraged in children of every ability, broadening the number of opportunities for achievement as well as for praise. That's not to say that intellectual achievement should go unpraised – of course not; all areas of development need to be encouraged.

One US study, by the National Center for Biotechnology Information, discovered that students in fifth grade (in the UK, equivalent to 11- and 12-year-olds in Year 7) gained more motivation from praise for *effort* than they did from praise for intelligence or talent. If they felt they'd failed after having been praised for their intelligence or talent, they would show less persistence and less enjoyment when repeating the same task; if, on the other hand, it was their *effort* that had been praised before the apparent failure, they would try again with renewed effort and do better. The children described intelligence and talent as being fixed traits, but believed that there was always scope for improvement in effort, and so greater scope for success and reward. The findings are a good illustration of how achievement is best encouraged when the praise is applied to effort over intellectual ability or natural flair.

Lucy has never been the brightest in her year group, but she's always been a trier. At her school the teachers award house points and stickers for effort as well as grades for academic achievement. It's made the transition from primary to high school less intimidating and makes her feel it's worth making the effort.

Rachael, mum to Lucy, 11

PRAISING EFFECTIVELY

So how can we apply these principles to everyday life, beginning when our children are young? Well, if your pre-school child successfully builds a tall tower of bricks, for example, or sorts all their shapes or colours correctly, instead of saying 'What a *clever child*!', try saying 'Well done – you've tried *really* hard, haven't you?'. Chances are, instead of resting back on their laurels, thinking 'Yes, I *am* clever, aren't I? Job done!', they'll try even harder to outdo themselves and gain more praise from you in the process. There's nothing at all wrong with telling them they're clever, too, from time to time; just keep in mind that cleverness, like beauty or height, is to a large extent a gift that your child has been born with rather than earned through effort, so isn't particularly praiseworthy in itself.

My two boys are so different in intellectual ability you'd think they were raised by different families, but they both really try hard. It can be hard not to compare Evan, who's five, with Daniel, now seven, especially when friends and relatives tend to ask where the boys are in their school years in terms of ability, and already Evan realizes he's not as bright as his big brother. At first, my husband and I used to heap praise on Daniel, because when he was the only one at school there were no direct comparisons being made. But now Evan is in Year 1, we're doing our best to praise them equally, focusing on effort. Now, instead of saying to Daniel 'Who's a bright boy, then?' which would leave Evan a bit crestfallen, we say 'Well done, Dan, you gave it your best!'. Then, when Evan brings home a piece of work, we can say the same sort of thing to him. And when friends and family single out Daniel's cleverness, we balance their comments by pointing out that both boys are equally committed to putting in a good effort.

Chloe, mum to Daniel, seven, and Evan, five

Insight

You can give your children an equal sense of achievement at home by setting each of them daily tasks involving effort, and setting up a reward scheme such as a star chart. Split the tasks into age relevance: your toddler could tidy their toys away into a box morning and evening; your school-age child could keep their book bag in order or fold some of the washing. Perhaps have column headings like 'Good try', for a less-than-enthusiastic but compliant approach; 'Brilliant effort' for a job done willingly; and 'Superstar!' for efforts beyond the call of duty! Three stars in any column could earn them a small reward.

The importance of praise by age

Praise equals motivation and confidence – and different strategies work best with different age groups. Clapping your hands and enthusing 'Good girl!' may make your three-year-old brim with pride, but is unlikely to be as well received by your ten-year-old. An important point to keep in mind is that children, by and large, like to feel they're achieving something a bit 'grown up' for their age. At every age and stage, it's common to find children metaphorically trying to run before they can walk (and we as adults can be equally guilty in certain circumstances, too – it's all part of the human condition). So helping your child to keep their goals in perspective while making slightly more challenging things achievable for them will boost their self-esteem and encourage them to take the next step – but only when they're good and ready.

Insight

It may seem obvious that praise should be linked to age, but too often we simply deliver the same old standbys, whatever the child's maturity. As your child grows in understanding, it's a good thing to elaborate on your praise, even if it's after the event.

YOUR BABY

It's never too early to start helping your child achieve some goals, as long as they are realistic and age-appropriate, and you can even start in babyhood. Once your baby is obviously responding to you – by watching and mimicking your facial expressions or laughing along when you amuse them, for example – you can show them a new skill and encourage them to try it too. The opportunities for praise are almost endless!

▶ Once they're babbling, open up the idea of conversation by chatting to them, then pausing to allow them time to respond. In encouraging tones, you can then reply saying something that lends itself to enthusiastic delivery, like 'Are you talking to Mummy? Isn't it fun having little chats with each other?' Your baby will glean a lot from your facial expressions and the tone and inflection of your voice, and will soon crack on to the fact that you're pleased with their efforts.

▶ Similarly, once they're able to sit unsupported, you can place their favourite toys just out of reach and encourage them as they stretch to grab them.

▶ Then, when they're old enough, you can ask them to point at pictures in their best board book or touch their own nose, eyes and mouth.

We couldn't get over it when Hattie spontaneously touched her own nose as I was telling her mum that mine felt really itchy! She was only 14 months old at the time and I had no idea she had so much understanding of language. That started off a new game between us when I would say 'Where's Hattie's tummy?' or 'Where are Daddy's eyes?' and she would mostly respond correctly. Her face was a picture when she got a question right. We still play this when I get in from work, and she'll give herself a little clap whenever I say 'Yes, that's right!'

Laurence, dad to Hattie, 18 months

YOUR TODDLER

If your pre-schooler is in childcare, they should be achieving goals regularly, as all early years providers in the UK have to follow the Early Years Foundation Stage (EYFS) network of learning as laid down by the government for babies and children from birth to age five.

This means that as well as looking after children from babyhood onwards, all formal child carers also have to take an active part in their development and early learning. Ask your childcare provider to explain how they're fulfilling the EYFS curriculum, and ask them to keep a daily log of your child's achievements so you can encourage your child in the same way.

At home, too, you can give your toddler opportunities to build up their confidence through early achievement and praise for their efforts.

▶ Set up an art area where they can give vent to their creativity: lay out a piece of plastic sheeting, fixing it to the floor with masking tape; provide some washable paints, some PVA glue, and some pieces of tissue or fabric for them to use in a collage. Help them to think about how they might use the materials, and chat to them about their design as they go along – it'll make them feel they're achieving something worthwhile, boost their confidence and encourage them in their efforts.

▶ Give them some paper napkins to lay out on the table when it's time for tea, and don't forget to say 'Thank you for helping Mummy.' Feeling that their contribution is actually helpful can give their self-esteem a big boost. (Resist the urge to go and rearrange the napkins if you're a perfectionist; this will have the opposite effect and invalidate their effort. In fact, it's a good time to learn to keep your perfectionism to yourself!)

▶ Give them a flannel to wash themselves with in the bath. Don't leave them unsupervised, but don't interfere either, unless it's to play with them. Once you've shampooed their hair, give them a plastic cup or jug to start the rinsing with. Although you'll have to finish the job for them, let them have the idea that they're doing the main part so they get a positive view of their own contribution.

▶ Make it easier for them to start doing other simple things for themselves: place some step stools wherever appropriate – in front of the basin, for example – but obviously not close to any potential dangers. They'll feel very independent being able to get to places without always being lifted into position, then relying on someone for a lift back down again – and it's good preparation for pre-school too.

I was terribly guilty of doing absolutely everything for Robert: I thought it would be quicker and that I'd do a better job, to be honest. Then one of the leaders at his playgroup pointed out that Robert was very capable of brushing his own hair and putting his own coat on, given a little bit of encouragement and enough time, and she explained how proud he was of sticking his own paintings on the wall with sticky putty. I started letting him do stuff for himself more at home and he went from strength to strength in no time. Now he puts his own slippers and dressing gown on and off, brings his empty sipper cup out to the kitchen for a refill and turns his own nightlight on at night. I think I feel even prouder than he does, and praise comes very naturally as a result!

Selina, mum to Robert, two and a half

YOUR OLDER CHILD

School-age children can gain great benefit from becoming more independent, and your child's teachers and other carers will appreciate it if they have certain practical and social skills in place. They may not be aware of just how much they can try to do for themselves – or they may think they can take greater leaps forward than they can actually manage. Whatever their level of confidence now, giving them achievable goals, then praising their efforts, will increase their feelings of self-esteem and give them greater confidence to try new things. Try to encourage 'I can' thinking wherever appropriate, rather than allowing them to feel that they need to rely on you for everything. It'll boost their self-esteem, too, if you let them practise something they're already good at before taking on a new challenge.

There are lots of ways you can challenge your child to achieve small goals, and the more small things they achieve, the more they'll want to try.

▶ Show them how you lay the table, and then let them have a go at placing the cutlery. Don't correct them straight away if they get things in the wrong order or give someone two forks by mistake; praise them for having a go, and say something like 'You'll soon be able to do it without me, I can tell!' Next time, show them again, and then let them try, and continue like this until they master it.

▶ Listen to them read every day. Their schoolteacher should be encouraging this, but you can also provide age-appropriate titles at home and practise with them (using whichever method their school prefers so as not to confuse them and cause their confidence to plummet). Rather than correcting their every mistake, simply repeat words that they get wrong, so that they remember them for next time.

▶ Let them have a say, within reason, in how things are arranged in their room. If they want their cuddly toys all over their bed, ask them to arrange them each day; if they want their pictures displayed on their walls or cupboard doors, make some blank space for them (and find a way of fixing them that won't leave permanent marks, unless you're likely to redecorate any time soon!); provide a small piece of furniture or other storage for them to fill with whatever they like – it could be a toy box, plastic crate, bookshelf, small set of drawers or cupboard.

▶ Let them help make their packed lunch or tea. There are lots of no-cook things they could do, like spreading the butter on the rolls, arranging a salad, chopping soft fruit with a blunt knife or wrapping their sandwiches up. Avoid only saying 'Clever child!', and praise their efforts more specifically: 'You've got to have a good eye to spread butter as evenly as that' or 'What a great job you've made of that salad – it looks very tempting.'

Sangeeta is turning into a proper little helper since I gave her her own list of jobs to do. She knows it's her responsibility to put her own shoes and uniform out ready for school, clear the table after tea, and dry up any plastic things from the washing up and empty her school lunchbox every day. She's got a little dusting kit in her bedroom too (her idea, not mine!), and she's such a keen little worker that we got her an apron of her own, which she puts on at the first sign of a job needing doing. Long may it last – although I suspect it won't!

Poonam, mum to Sangeeta, seven

YOUR TWEENIE

Children at that 'in between' age are almost on a par with teenagers when it comes to which group tries hardest to push boundaries. It seems as if today's tweenies have higher expectations of freedom than ever before. So how do we, as parents, allow them enough flexibility without losing control? And how do we strike a balance between wrapping them up in cotton wool and letting go, especially as our actions will have a bearing on their confidence? The key is to strike compromises with your child: don't dismiss all their requests out of hand, but see if you can find a halfway point of agreement. On the plus side, it'll give you plenty of scope for praise when they don't step over the mark.

▶ Agree that your tween can go to the cinema with their friends unescorted, but only on the understanding that you or another parent drop them off and pick them up afterwards. Help them feel more empowered by giving them some money to spend on food and drink, and let them make her own choices. Afterwards tell them how proud of them you are – they've acted responsibly and earned more freedom by not abusing your trust.

▶ Allow your child to go on a shopping trip with mates in town on the proviso that you are also shopping in the vicinity so that you're on hand to respond to any emergencies or crises. Arrange a time and place to meet them later on (checking first that their mobile is charged, in credit and showing the correct time!). Don't keep calling their mobile to see where they are or remind them of the time; let them know you trust them, and that as long as they comply this time there'll be opportunities for more outings. Acknowledge their responsibility when they meet you at (or around) the agreed time. Suggest another upcoming opportunity when they can enjoy the same privileges, so that they link their cooperation to a further reward.

▶ Agree to consider extending your child's bedtime – but only once you have evidence that they're getting sufficient sleep, i.e. they wake easily and get up fairly readily when called on school mornings. It's best, for several reasons, to start with a bedtime that's 15 minutes later than usual and take it from there: first, because it's hard to backtrack if you give them an extension of half an hour and then find it's too much for them; second, because you'll keep back more bargaining power for later on; third, because too late a bedtime for your child will mean less of an evening for you! (Time enough for the further intrusion when your child hits teenage years.) As long as they're still coping well with their homework and don't come home exhausted, you can reinforce that it was a good decision to allow them a later bedtime, which will make them feel more grown up.

▶ Instigate other small freedoms. Let them take their bike to the local park with friends; if you have a nearby shop, send them round for a few items of shopping; if school is within walking distance, encourage them to meet a friend and go without you. (Starting in summer months is a good idea – perhaps during the term before they start high school.) Each time they behave responsibly – by texting you to say they're on their way home, turning up on time or spotting a good bargain when you send them food shopping – make sure you acknowledge and praise their effort. Too often we focus on misbehaviour and forget to praise for expected obedience – but don't forget that with independent thinking comes freedom of choice, so good behaviour should earn a positive response from you.

▶ Make them feel capable and important. If they have a younger sibling, for example, ask for their help with bath time or supper time; get them to read a bedtime story; or help your younger child change into pyjamas. Maybe you could reward them with a little extra pocket money if they agree to take on one or more of these responsibilities on a regular basis.

Kristina has always been a bit cosseted because she's an only child and I'm a single parent, so I guess I've found it harder to let go than other parents might. I realized recently that she's the only kid in her class (or so it seems) that doesn't have a mobile phone so I let her buy a cheapie with her own money and I've started going halves with her on pay-as-you-go top-ups every month – but only if she uses her credit wisely. She's chuffed to bits to be in charge of such a grown-up item, and she can't abuse it because she's not allowed to buy any extra credit for herself so she has to manage it to a budget. It's a good exercise in self-restraint, but also independent thinking.

Marina, mum to Kristina, ten

YOUR TEEN

Once they have reached teenage years, most kids are fairly adept at getting what they want, but it doesn't mean they're full of confidence. Teenage years, you may remember, are a stage when crises of confidence often arise. Each child is trying to find their own identity and may be struggling with all sorts of issues like body image, sexuality and likes/dislikes. You'll notice more pronounced mood swings (unless you're very fortunate) and you may find yourself the target of your teenager's rages and insolence. In some ways, teen behaviour can be a bit like toddler unruliness: anger when they try and fail; frustration with themselves; looking for someone to take hurt feelings out on; a need to be able to regress a little in a safe environment; needing endless patience and understanding!

When the going gets tough, remind yourself that you came through that phase and you can get through this one too. What your child needs now more than ever is constancy, unconditional love and plenty of support, and it's your job to find reserves of all of these, even when they seem in pretty short supply!

Too much correction (except where it's really necessary), disapproval or hostility will probably result in a breakdown in communication between you – which is the opposite of what you both need throughout the teen years. OK, so you may not enjoy long, one-to-one, sit-down chats as your child matures from a child to a young adult, but you do need to know – as do they – that lines of communication are always open, and that there is scope for discussion, no matter what the topic of conversation.

Don't beat yourself up if you do lose your temper sometimes; we're all only human and the odd outburst is unlikely to do any lasting damage – if anything, it'll show your child that everyone has a breaking point and it might even help them see things from your point of view. If you think it's appropriate, then apologize (and even if you don't think so, it might help get things back to normal more quickly), then try not to interfere too much or become overly obsessed with your teen's emotional state – it'll probably settle. At the same time, step up the level of independence appropriate to your teenager's age. They might not want to take on some of the following suggestions, but it's time to explain to them that growing up is all about give as well as take. In any case, if you load the chores with the odd reward for doing them properly and loads of praise for a good result, it'll help sweeten the pill.

▶ Show them how to do their own laundry. You can decide how far to go with this, for example, are you happy with them sorting the loads themselves? Will you settle for having the washing loaded and started or do you want them to hang it out afterwards as well? (One step at a time might be the best approach or you could all end up feeling it's more trouble than it's worth.)

▶ Let them take charge of their own grooming. (If you have a son, set up with him up with a good razor, hair products and other toiletries, then leave him to get on with preening if he wants to. Basic hygiene you might need to encourage, though!) Don't go over the top with praise about your teen's appearance; that may be the last thing they want from you! A throw-away compliment like 'Looking good' is more than adequate unless they actually ask for your opinion. But do tell them they've done well to get ready quickly or thank them for putting their toiletries away or keeping the bathroom tidy.

▶ If they're happy for you to choose their clothes, fair enough, but if they have their own style, give them some money to go shopping and kit themselves out. Start with small amounts of money until they've proven they won't lose or squander it, but remember this exercise is about building their confidence through trust, so praise them when they use money wisely.

▶ Let them have their privacy. Agree to you knocking before you go into their room (and ask that they do the same for you). If there's dirty washing, or dirty plates and mugs, to be brought downstairs, give them a chance to bring them themselves, then tell them you'll be going in there in half an hour, to give them a chance to put away anything personal. Don't pry unless you have cause to think they're getting themselves into trouble; it might disturb you to think your teen's exploring things an adult would enjoy, but that's a normal part of growing up and shouldn't concern you as long as it's nothing dangerous. Talk to them regularly about staying safe online and the dangers of dabbling in drugs, but try not to preach; if you want to stay in the picture they need to feel they can talk openly without being judged.

▶ Keep in mind that if their room is their sanctuary, they're more likely to spend time at home than if you insist on invading their space and dictating how it should look. Thank them for any effort at tidying or cleaning their room, and show them that you appreciate their time with you at home (even if they do spend it barricaded into their room or texting their mates).

I learned my lesson when Katy suddenly wanted to sleep over at friends' houses every weekend – and I realized that she wasn't too chuffed about being at home during the week either. At first when I questioned her she just said 'It's what teenagers

*do, Mum' in her most patronizing tones, but then we got into
a row about something else and she came out with a whole lot
of stuff about how no teenager would want to live in our house
with the amount of butting in I apparently do. I'm a single
parent, so I do get a bit lonely at weekends, and I admit I did
used to try and get involved whenever she had friends over,
bringing them drinks and snacks every half hour and asking
them what they were up to. Anyway I'm glad we fell out really,
because it gave us a chance to clear the air and lay some new
rules (mostly for me!). Now I leave her some pizzas and drinks
in the fridge to sort out for herself and her friends, and I retire to
the living room with a good DVD and a glass of wine, or have
some friends of my own round. I'm learning to get on with the
divide between me and them, and Katy is happier to be here now.
She appreciates that leaving her alone means I trust her more.*

Lucy, mum to Katy, 15

YOUNG ADULT

If your child is still living with you at age 18, and has no plans to go
off to university, you might feel you've got no more rights over them
now they're an adult. That's not true, though: if they were living in
rented accommodation, they'd have to abide by some house rules,
and the same applies if they're going to remain at home. It doesn't
mean treating them like a tenant, though. Of course, you'll want
them to continue to take part in family life; the tricky part is getting
the right balance.

▶ Have a think about which rules are most important to you,
and then talk them through with them so they feel you're
communicating on equal terms. If you think they should ask
before borrowing the family car, for instance, say so, but don't
hide the keys from them as that'll suggest you don't trust them –
leave them in their usual place and ask them just to clear it with
you first. Discuss what will happen if they decide spontaneously
to stay out all night – if they were living independently you'd
have no idea they hadn't come home, but you'll want to know
whether or not you can lock up for the night, so it's a matter of
courtesy for them to keep you informed. (And do thank them for
letting you know – that's important.)

- ▶ Decide between you whether or not you'll continue to food shop for them or whether they'd rather have their own shelf in the fridge and sort themselves out. Praise any effort at self-catering, even if it's only shoving a pizza in the oven. Encourage them to clear away after themselves, and then thank them for doing so.
- ▶ If they're earning, come to an agreement about how much they'll contribute to the family finances. Work out a reasonable percentage of their income rather than charging them the going rate for rented accommodation (unless you really want them to move out!). Discuss ways of ensuring they pay you regularly: could they set up a standing order, for instance?
- ▶ Once they're contributing to the household, it's important you treat them like an equal adult, while understanding that they may still have a lot to learn about responsibility. Involve them in discussions about budgeting and spending, and show your appreciation for any ideas they come up with.
- ▶ If they're not earning, it's a good idea to give them an allowance each month. It'll mean they can still make decisions about when and what to spend (including buying you presents if they want to), rather than having to ask for money each time they need it. And it'll help them manage money too – especially if you're not too ready with the extra hand-outs when they run short.

Drawing up a nominal financial agreement with Ewan has actually made him feel more adult and independent than if we'd just continued supporting him without it costing him a penny. We don't want to make his student debt even worse, so we don't ask much of him, but if he wants to borrow the car we ask for some contribution to the petrol, and he also pays a small amount towards his insurance. It's good training as he'll have to support himself and manage his debt when he does eventually leave home for good.

Angela, mum to Ewan, 19

Insight

Having your child with you in young adulthood will bring its own challenges, and you might feel like you should distance yourself a bit so that your child has enough privacy. But don't take things too far: you're still a family and there should still be opportunities for family fun. What about suggesting you all go out for a pub lunch every month or planning the odd weekend away together?

How praise can have a negative impact

It might sound unlikely, but there are situations where praise can actually have a negative effect, particularly on older children. As they mature, children begin to interpret praise – and the motivation behind it – in more and more sophisticated ways. So, for instance, they can feel very patronized if given too much praise for a small achievement. It's useful to try and remember this as your child grows. For example, instead of saying: 'What a wonderful picture – that's the best I've ever seen you do! Where did you get all that artistic talent from?' you could be much more specific and slightly less effusive so that your child will appreciate the point you're actually making. For instance: 'What I really like about this picture is the perspective' or 'Your use of colour is really coming on.' They're much more likely to appreciate that you do think their work is good, and you'll have given them an important confidence boost.

Praise can also be seen in a negative light if your child senses that you're using it to manipulate them, and this can make them deliberately disruptive: it's their way of proving they can see through you and know your motives, or showing you that they've got more understanding than you give them credit for. The trouble is recognizing the effect; better to avoid the situation by trying to keep in mind your child's level of mental sophistication when you choose how to praise. (Easier said than done, but it comes with practice.)

Children do reach an age where they're able to judge their own progress and accomplishments pretty well for themselves. According to Jennifer Henderlong Corpus and Mark Lepper, US psychologists who have analysed over 30 years of studies on the effects of praise, children associate insincere praise with the feeling that their parents don't really know or understand them. It's another case for keeping praise specific and in proportion to the achievement, and underlines a previous point that praise for effort is more important than praising natural intelligence.

Insight

If the five-to-one praise-to-criticism ratio sounds like it might set you up to sound insincere all over again, remember that praise doesn't have to be effusive and can include lots of different appreciative comments like: 'Oh, you've changed into your pyjamas already – well done'; 'Good boy, you've eaten all your dinner'; 'I like those shoes with those trousers'; or 'Thanks for taking your plate out to the kitchen.'

Ways children seek approval

Children seek approval in various ways depending on their individual characters, and the ways they do it can apply at any age: some are happy to behave in a moderate, cooperative way for most of the time; others look for plenty of praise for the smallest effort; some equate approval with tangible rewards, such as a packet of sweets or extra pocket money. Sometimes, children who are lacking in praise exhibit undesirable attention-seeking behaviour and will misbehave deliberately, knowing that they will eventually gain approval for stopping, if nothing else.

THE 'YES' CHILD

The first scenario above of the largely cooperative child may sound ideal, but it's important to make sure that the child who's an apparent paragon of good behaviour isn't afraid to hold and voice their own opinions or to challenge adult rules if they can't see the sense in them. A 'yes' child may find it hard to speak up – or, worse, may feel intimidated by their parents' very high expectations of good behaviour to the extent that they feel to question them would be to step out of line. They may become so accepting of the home code of conduct that they perceive other families' ways of going about things as wrong. They may grow up afraid of confrontation of any sort, and this in turn could lead them to making or tolerating unsuitable relationships in their efforts to please and never disappoint.

Having a very compliant child may make for an easier life for you, but imagine this trait translated into classroom behaviour: the child who has no opinion at home is unlikely to understand how to formulate one outside of the home either, and may be unable to contribute to classroom debates or to question theories or see things from the opposite viewpoint. They'll probably be reluctant to disagree with a given statement, even when this is what the teacher's looking for, and this could in turn undermine their confidence in their own thought processes.

Lee's Year 6 teacher was quite frustrated with his inability to express a preference about anything in class. She said she'd asked him various different things like whether he preferred learning by doing practical experiments or by reading instructions – which was an important consideration – and he just said he didn't mind

*either way. The same thing happened when they were discussing
books and DVDs, and when she asked him what his favourite
subject was. We realized we weren't really encouraging him
to speak out at home, and I think it's a by-product of my own
parents being quite Victorian in their approach to child-rearing.
We were very much to be seen but not heard, which was very
old-fashioned given that I grew up in the 1970s! Now we're
encouraging Lee more by giving him options for what to eat for
dinner or what to wear at the weekend – and it's only when he's
made a choice that his mum will go ahead and dig his clothes out
or make tea. It's gradually having an effect, although it's meant a
couple of spats with his younger siblings who've got used to him
letting them watch whatever they want on television and so on.
But I think that's a good thing actually, because he'll have to hold
his own at high school next year.*

Darren, dad to Lee, 11, Zach, nine and Lois, seven

Insight

The best approach when teaching children how to express their opinions is to
do it in a way that avoids open confrontation where possible. It's more about
teaching your child negotiating skills than showing them that whoever shouts
loudest gets their own way.

THE PRIMA DONNA

If your child behaves like a prima donna expecting to be praised to
the hilt for every tiny achievement, try playing down the over-the-top
praise and offer kisses, cuddles and high fives in its place. Explain to
your child that approval can be expressed in all sorts of ways, either
verbally or physically, and it's all equally valid. Eventually your child
will be happy with 'Great job!' or 'Thanks for doing that,' which
will stand them in good stead for when they're cooperating away
from home.

One danger of over-the-top praise being handed out on a regular
basis is that your child may feel they're achieving so well that there's
no room for improvement. Also, they may begin to feel like a failure
at school when their best efforts aren't met with rows of gold stars
or a full complement of house points every time, and when other
peers outperform compared with them. And, of course, at those times
when they do fail at anything, their fall will be harder than the child
whose parents have kept the praise in proportion; that's because the

child with realistic expectations of praise in line with achievement will also have a more balanced approach to disappointment.

It took me a while to strike the right balance of praise with Eva. I used to sound ridiculously proud now I think back, gushing about her every achievement. Then when she couldn't do something first time round she'd just give up and start saying she was useless at it. I can see I made a rod for my own back there. Now I get her to try new things and I coach her and encourage her at the same time. I've also told her about all the stuff it took me ages to learn how to do, and I tell her it's worth all the failures when you eventually manage to master something as it feels like a much bigger achievement.

Ally, mum to Eva, five

Insight

One important aspect of confidence-building in children is to show them that it's quite normal – and perfectly acceptable – to fail at things. The best way of demonstrating this is by coping well with your own failures. Allowing ourselves and our children to fail without criticism gives us all the self-esteem to push ourselves, confident in the knowledge that to fail is OK and that the best option is to have another go.

THE DEMANDING HELPER

If you have a child who equates approval with reward, the potential stumbling block is that they could be reluctant to cooperate unless there's an obvious pay-off, and the logical next step is for you to bribe them into helping. In this case, setting up a reward-earning scheme, like a star chart where every set of five stars gains them a treat, is a good idea; so is offering cuddles, extra story time, and the promise of 15 minutes' play time with you or some other non-material prize.

With an older child or teenager, the situation can turn on its head as the nature of rewards changes: for instance, freedoms can only be earned once your child has proven their own trustworthiness. So if they want to be allowed to go regularly to a local music gig, for example, they need to demonstrate a sense of responsibility by fulfilling pre-agreed conditions like coming home at the appointed time. It's equally important that you acknowledge them cooperating, though, so don't forget to say 'Great, you're back on time. That means I'm happy to let you go again,' rather than ignoring the fact that they've kept their side of the bargain. Giving them the feeling that you haven't particularly noticed they're home on time could backfire with them trying to push the boundaries next time to see what they can get away with.

Joshua was never the sort of child to follow the crowd and was always happy to do as we asked him, but when he got to being a teenager he started taking his freedom for granted and expecting to be dropped off and picked up at all sorts of times of day. We'd given him free rein to go out with his mates and he seemed to think it was his right rather than a privilege! We decided he'd only be able to go out at weekends and only then if he'd done something to earn it. At first he was quite cross but when he realized his freedom depended on it he started to think more about how he could help us more, and now he's back on track, so everyone's happy.

Geri, mum to Joshua, 13

THE ATTENTION SEEKER

A child who misbehaves deliberately is usually craving attention – be it positive or negative – and this shows they're feeling a little bit neglected or ignored. It's too easy as parents for us to overlook good behaviour and only point out the bad stuff, and it takes an extra effort on our part to remember to praise when things are going as we would like and expect. But children do need reassurance and acknowledgement for effort, even it it's just for not arguing back or for doing as they're told. When a child would clearly prefer a telling-off to no reaction from you, it's important to remember that they're accepting this as the next-best option to being praised; they're really in need of more positive attention. Remember the golden rule of trying to give five times as much praise as criticism, and make it a habit to acknowledge small things throughout the day, even those that don't require specific praise: 'Thanks' when they throw rubbish in the bin; 'That's nice' if they stroke the family pet; 'Well done' when they hand you something you've asked them to find; 'I love you' wherever, whenever and for no apparent reason – all of these tiny positive affirmations will add to their growing bank of confidence.

Amy was so demanding of my approval that it became really awkward when we were out together. She'd unload some of the shopping on to the conveyor belt in the supermarket and go on and on about it, saying 'Am I a good girl, Mummy?' or 'That little girl isn't helping her mummy. She's not good like me, is she?' continuously. It became exhausting and embarrassing to listen to until it my mum suggested that perhaps Amy actually wanted me to notice her efforts without having to point them out. I started praising her more, albeit in a very low-key way, and it didn't take long before I noticed her becoming much less demanding. It makes perfect sense now I think about it, but it took for my mum to see it as an outsider.

Leah, mum to Amy, six

Insight

Your child will pick up on how you behave towards other members of the family and your friends as well as them – and if you constantly praise their efforts but take others for granted, they could get mixed messages as well as an over-inflated idea of their importance within the family.

Why children deliberately wind us up

As well as the reasons described above, where the child is happier with negative attention than no attention at all, a degree of insecurity can also result in disruptive behaviour as children 'test' their parents by trying to flout the rules. A framework of rules where there are clear boundaries about what's acceptable and what isn't will make a child feel secure and reinforce the idea that their parents are in control. (Read more about this in the next chapter.) Once they're sure you're not going to cave in under their misbehaviour they'll feel reassured that there are limits to what they can get away with, which in turn tells them that you're looking out for them and that they'll be safely looked after. This is why it's important to stand by the house rules as far as possible – and, if you do decide to bend them on occasion, to give a good explanation as to why, as well as reiterating that it's a one-off.

There's another reason why children deliberately wind their parents up too: it's another way of asserting their own independence and, if handled sensitively, can actually help to boost confidence. Sometimes it can be a sign, for example, that your child is growing out of some of the old house rules, and you may need to have another look at them. If, for instance, you find your older child trying to make themselves a drink in a glass beaker when previously they've only been allowed a plastic cup, it may be that they're actually ready to progress. In this case, their behaviour isn't naughty, just a bit adventurous, and you should support it.

The same applies if, for instance, you've always insisted on their holding your hand when you cross the road: if they suddenly start to shrug you off and try to cross independently, it could be they're ready for a little more responsibility. A good way to handle either situation is to ask yourself whether or not your child has a valid point, then show them the safest way forward, for example, get them to put the glass on a steady surface and hold it with both hands when carrying it to and from the kitchen. Let them practise crossing minor roads near your home while you supervise, then get them to take the lead whenever you're out together, telling you when they think it's safe for you both to cross. Sometimes our children grow and develop skills more quickly than we recognize, and it can take a little bit of healthy negotiation to help them move on safely.

How to handle over-confidence

Sometimes children can appear over-confident, bragging, showing off and generally trying to steal the limelight. But before you think you've spoilt your child with too much praise, ask yourself if there's anything this behaviour could be masking. As with adults, the child who pushes herself forward is often lacking in self-esteem or craving more attention. So instead of trying to knock them off their perch or bring them down a peg, think about how you can invest a little bit more time in one-to-one attention.

TIPS FOR ALL AGES

Although toddlers and primary-school age kids tend to show off more than older children, it's not a trait exclusive to this age group, and it can be just because they're so proud of their own achievements. But if your child is becoming insufferable or embarrassing to take out because of their constant stealing of the limelight from their peers or showing off in front of adults, it may be that they're not getting quite enough recognition or that their self-esteem could do with a boost. You can apply and adapt the following tips to all age groups.

▶ Give them plenty of low-key praise for small achievements as well as greater ones. Acknowledge little things like sharing a toy with their sibling, spontaneously giving you a kiss, clearing the table without complaint or saying 'thank you' without being reminded.

▶ If you've found it hard to give them special time each day, try to fit in at least 10 minutes of one-to-one attention where you have no distractions and just play, cuddle, read or chat together. This is equally important with older, more independent children as well as with youngsters.

▶ Point out others' achievements without denigrating their own.

▶ Give them constructive criticism as well as unconditional praise; there's usually room for improvement, and as long as you praise first, there's nothing wrong with offering tips for doing better next time. For example, if they're learning a musical instrument, you could comment on their practice: 'That piece sounds technically great. Maybe next time you could try it with a little more emotion to make it even better.'

▶ Remind them that not all children are as able as they are, but many try equally hard. Explain that effort is just as praiseworthy, if not more so, as final achievement.

10 THINGS TO REMEMBER

1 Even a baby can gain confidence from the tone and inflection of your voice when you encourage them.

2 Try to ignore unimportant misbehaviour and focus on praising your child when they're good.

3 Be specific with your praise so your child is in no doubt as to how they've pleased you.

4 Set your child challenging but fairly easy to achieve goals so they feel proud of their own abilities.

5 Show them it's OK to fail by highlighting the times when you could have done better, and laughing at yourself.

6 Keep your praise appropriate to their level of achievement and age so they doesn't feel patronized.

7 Encourage them to practise something they're already good at before they tackle a new, more difficult challenge.

8 Encourage your child to formulate and voice their own opinions, and show them how to put their point of view across without becoming confrontational.

9 Listen to them, and repeat back key information they have shared with you so that they know you've listened properly.

10 Review your house rules from time to time and take your lead from them when they seem ready for more responsibility.

3

Confidence building at home

In this chapter you will learn:
- *how rules and boundaries increase confidence*
- *the role of position within the family*
- *how to give your child appropriate responsibilities*
- *how to teach your child to take pride in their work.*

The role of family life

Simply being part of a family – however small or large – means your child is part of a team and will have to learn team skills, which will be hugely useful to them in the wider world. The larger the family, the quicker they'll pick these up – and, to some extent, they may come more naturally to children in larger families; but smaller families still need to learn to co-operate in order to live happily together. If your family is small but you involve wider family and friends as often as you can, your child will get the chance to interact with adults and children of different ages, and they'll learn to behave in different ways as a result. This can teach a lot about responsibility, trust and respect. So how can you encourage great team play within the family?

Insight
Families with an only child are still a team. As parents you need to be mindful that your child doesn't have the benefit of an older sibling's encouragement or practical help, and that they don't have the same sense of responsibility that comes with having a younger brother or sister, so it's up to you to find ways to encourage teamwork.

YOUR BABY

OK, so an infant may not be able to grasp the concept of teamwork, but being at the centre of the family when everyone is co-operating around them – and getting used to their demands being met by more than just mum – will help your baby to grow up with the idea that everyone works together to make the cogs of the family wheel run smoothly.

▶ Encourage everyone in the family to take turns looking after and chatting to the baby of the family.

▶ Let your baby witness you sharing chores, mealtimes, conversations and treats.

▶ Socialize them with visitors if they seem willing – but you may notice clingy behaviour creeping in for a few months from around seven months old. This is perfectly normal and coincides with the realization that they are, in fact, separate from you and therefore vulnerable. It can continue for several months until your baby grasps the concept of 'object permanence' – that is, that an object or person can still exist even when it is out of their sight. (Playing games like Peek-A-Boo can help them get to grips with this idea.) Until this stage, every time you disappear your baby will think you've gone for good – no wonder they panic!

At first we had a highchair for Amelia, but the tray was so large that she was always set too far back from the table when we had meals. Then we bought one of those seats that clips on to the edge of a table for when we were going on holiday, and it involved her so much more that we started using it at home, too. We have a sturdy wooden kitchen table it screwed on to securely, and suddenly Amelia was much more involved in mealtimes, reaching out to try some of our food as well as trying to share her own!

Dorinda, mum to Amelia, 14 months, and pregnant with twins

YOUR TODDLER

It'll still be a bit beyond your toddler to play a full role within the family team, but you can continue the good work of showing them how life goes more smoothly when you all co-operate with each other. They might be a bit prone to tantrums as they grow in independence and try to assert themselves. You can seize the best moments for getting them to co-operate by avoiding times when they're tired, hungry, thirsty, bored or under the weather. When they're on good form, there are a few things you can encourage them to do.

▶ Make a regular time to get all the family involved in simple board games and other activities that require a team of people. Get your child to hand out pens, playing tokens, cards and whatever else is needed. Learning to take turns is an important part of working as part of a team, so don't be too tempted to let them have 'just one more go' if they're falling behind in the game. Instead explain that everyone takes turns to win and lose and it's all part of playing games.

▶ You might want to turn a blind eye to a dodgy move here and there in a family game – especially if you think it might avert a tantrum – but don't let your child get away with too much cheating; they need to learn that everyone's on an equal footing and that fair play is an important discipline within a family.

▶ Encourage them to put all their building bricks or jigsaw pieces away while you do some other chore like sorting the washing.

▶ If they'd rather help you with your own chore, ask them to pass you items of laundry to pair up, or pass you the pegs as you hang washing on the line.

▶ When you're clearing away after a meal, pass them things to put in the bin, like paper napkins, empty yogurt pots and so on.

▶ If you're going out, ask them to take their own slippers off and put them away somewhere tidy while you find their shoes.

▶ On a family outing, let them help unpack the picnic and pass food round.

▶ Don't forget to thank them for helping and try to ignore any refusals – hard though it'll undoubtedly be!

▶ It's a great idea to use a reward chart for team play with this age group.

Daniel used to refuse to do anything I asked him to, throwing things down on the floor and kicking off in a big way. Then I thought of giving him a choice between three different things: for instance, he could start getting himself undressed for his bath, get his bath toys out or put some of his downstairs toys away. If he co-operated he could watch an extra cartoon or have his favourite story afterwards. It's working – at least for now – and, although I have to say it would be far easier for me to do everything for him, it's taught him that we all pull together, and it's made him feel useful, I think.

Liz, mum to Daniel, three

YOUR YOUNG CHILD

By the time your child reaches the rising-five stage, they can join in a bit more with family life, whether it's having fun playing board or team games or helping out with simple chores. Perhaps they could help with laying or clearing the table or maybe they could be the person responsible for asking people what drinks they want or putting fruit into the fruit bowl when you're unpacking the supermarket shopping. It'll all help make them feel very grown-up.

▶ Ask your child which jobs they think they could manage regularly – and have some contingencies they can swap them for if they become bored with the routine. Knowing they can do a job well without being nagged (although you may have to remind them from time to time) is great for their self-esteem.

▶ If your child has younger brothers or sisters, they'll get a real confidence boost by helping them out with things they can't manage yet, like putting their coats on, packing a couple of toys into a bag for the car, passing them a sipper cup or lifting them on or off low seats.

▶ When you're playing group games or sports, let your child take the lead as captain or chief organizer sometimes. It'll boost their confidence, as well as giving them a responsibility that doesn't have serious consequences!

▶ Show your child how to organize a team game when their friends come round. You could help them build an obstacle course in the garden or tell them how to set up a knock-out football competition.

Miriam is the youngest of three children and has a tendency to be quite bossy: she wants to organize the rest of us all the time. It puts the other kids' noses out of joint and isn't one of her most endearing qualities. Now we've come up with a system whereby we have a rota of who does which chores around the house. So if, for example, it's coming up to a mealtime, instead of Miriam automatically choosing to lay the table every time (which she loves) and telling the others what they're supposed to do, we have a rolling rota of Chief Table Layer, Water Pourer and

Clearer Away. That means no one's in charge and it's a proper mini democracy!

Anna, mum to Jack, nine, Lucy, seven and Miriam, five

Insight

Don't be afraid to let your young child lose in a team game – it's another worthwhile lesson in turn-taking. Getting used to losing or being a runner-up can actually boost their confidence for later on in life, as teaching them that it's OK not to come top in everything will allow them to take more risks without fear of losing face.

YOUR TWEENIE

It's a tough time being a tweenie, when you feel more grown-up than your years but you're not allowed as much freedom as you feel you could handle. So this is a great age to broaden your child's sense of responsibility at home and give him space to try new stuff within a safe, supervised environment. Depending on their age, where you live and their general maturity, you might have reached a stage where it would be OK for them to venture out locally on their own – maybe just to pop to the shops for you to begin with.

▶ Asking your child to go and buy something you need and coming back with the right change will give them a real sense of your trust and make them feel they're really helping you out.

▶ If this feels a bit beyond your child – or if you're just not comfortable with it yet – maybe you could both go to the shops, but they could buy something for you from one shop while you pop into another.

▶ It's a good time to involve your child in preparing the family's meals. If they're at high school, with any luck they'll be used to using a cooker and hob, so ask them what they're happy to do, whether it's making a simple pudding or peeling the vegetables, and let them get on with it. They might prefer you to be around, but there's no need to breathe down their neck.

▶ Your tweenie is likely to have a growing social life, and it will give them a big self-esteem boost if you can tell them some regular times when you'd be happy for them to invite friends round or arrange to go to their homes (with their parents' approval, of course). The condition must be that they double-check with you first and keep their mobile fully charged up and switched on; you could also build in a proviso that they do a chore in return. Maybe they could tidy or clean their room or the bathroom if they're expecting friends round, for instance.

Josephine is always wanting to go to the cinema with her friends and knows that most Saturday mornings are fine for her to meet up with them as long as she runs it by us first. She can easily walk there and, as long as we know what film she's seeing and when it finishes, I usually pick her and her mates up afterwards. If they want to spend extra time in town first, it's on the condition that she gets stuck in to some homework as soon as she gets in, or that she'll help out with the washing or some other chore. It's all about give and take and it's working – for now.

Connor, dad to Josephine, 12

Insight

Watch out for your child trying to push boundaries that are already quite lax enough. If, for example, you're relaxed about them going into town locally with friends on the condition that they get a certain bus home or that a parent collects them, don't let this suddenly turn into permission to go off further afield at will and under their own steam – unless, of course, you feel that they're ready for this. Children this age are experts at making you feel that quite a big next step is actually a tiny add-on to what they're already allowed to do. This is a good opportunity to go over the rules and boundaries again. They could just be testing the water to see whether you'll respond as they expect you to, or they could be feeling pressurized by their mates – and they might even be secretly relieved when you say no to something they're not really comfortable with themselves.

YOUR TEEN

There are few time periods when children are more self-obsessed than when they are teenagers, and it can be hard to get willing co-operation out of them. Rather than being at loggerheads all the time though, it can help build your teen's confidence as well as get them on board with family responsibilities if you gradually relax some of your rules. That's not to say you should take your eye off the ball, and you'll definitely need to make clear what the parameters are – as well as the consequences if they're not respected – but giving more small freedoms as your child develops shows them you trust them and that you see them as a responsible individual.

▶ Psychologists advise using positive affirmation to get desirable behaviour, and warn against giving children negative labels which often result in self-fulfilling prophecies. So, for instance, if you say to your teenager: 'I know you'll come home on time because you appreciate the freedom we're giving you to go out,' you're more likely to get cooperation than if you say: 'You'd better be back on time. I know what you're like – always trying to push your luck,' which will not only lower your child's self-esteem but might make them behave in the negative way you seem to expect from them.

▶ For every new freedom you give your child, introduce a new responsibility. This might be giving them their own bank account and cash card (overseen by you); it could be letting them set up a social networking page (but it's a good idea, in the interests of their safety, to make it a condition that you're one of their designated 'friends' so you can access their page from time to time); it could be something more family-orientated, such as regularly vacuming the house or cleaning the family's shoes. It'll give them a growing sense of confidence if they know they have ultimate responsibility for some areas of home life.

▶ Create a quiet study area where your child can do homework and revise for tests. It'll show them you understand that what they're doing is important.

▶ If they have siblings, make sure your teenager gets some private time. Maybe you could give them a sign to hang on the outside of their door letting other family members know they don't want to be disturbed, for instance. Let the others know it's very important the sign is respected, and explain that they'll get the same privilege when the time comes.

Giving Liam his privacy had a really good effect: after a couple of weeks, the novelty of holing himself up in his room all evening wore off and he started spending more time than ever with the rest of the family. I think just knowing he could escape and be alone if he wanted to was enough. We deliberately kept the family PC and television downstairs so he didn't have much to be upstairs for except his music. That won't change until he's left high school as it's too alienating and too much of a distraction having screen-based entertainment in the bedroom.

Hannah, mum to Liam, 14

Insight

At this age, most children are studying for exams and sometimes we can be guilty of bringing a bit too much pressure to bear on them. Parental encouragement is undoubtedly an important factor in motivating (not intimidating) them into applying themselves to their work, but it's just as important that we encourage them to cut loose and enjoy themselves sometimes.

YOUNG ADULT

By young adulthood your child will have broken away from the family to some degree or another, even if only in terms of going out more than they stay in. Even if they're at university though, as long as they're still based at home when they're not at college, they can stay involved in family life. Ways to boost their confidence will stem from training them to be completely independent and priming them for a life outside of the family home. You may feel a bit reluctant to equip them with all the skills to leave home because it's more comfortable for them to rely on you, but even if they remain with you for some time to come, they need to know that they could manage without you if they had to. The most important thing to bear in mind is that they are an adult – albeit a relatively inexperienced one – and that you need to communicate with them on adult terms. It's all about mutual respect at this stage, even though you're still very much their parent and will remain their parent.

▶ Encourage your child to think about their longer-term plans and let them know you're always available to listen to and discuss their views and ideas. Give feedback only if you're asked for it; sometimes a listening ear is all that's wanted.

▶ Support your child, even if their ideas seem a bit far-fetched. You could suggest they make a contingency arrangement in case their plans don't work out. Your support is vital to their self-esteem and will make them a happier, more confident person.

▶ Help your child to research ways of achieving their goals. It's disempowering for them if you refuse to become involved unless the goal is something you're keen on; being a good parent and building your child's confidence means always being there for them no matter what.

▶ They need to practise practical skills more than ever now if they're going to move towards complete independence. Show them how to cook some basic meals; budget for shopping and going out; plan ahead for ongoing costs like insurances and rent or mortgage payments; manage their own food by use-by dates and organize their own laundry.

We'd been expecting Lauren to go to university and follow her original plan to become an accountant, but she suddenly changed tack after her A levels and decided she wanted to pursue a career in dancing – something she's always had as a hobby. She's still trying to find a place at a dance school, but because she didn't go to a stage or performing arts high school I think her chances are a bit remote really. She's starting her own dance band with some local girls and they're trying to get bookings for performances now. Our attitude has been to let her take a year off from studies to get it out of her system and keep her at home for another year in the hope she'll go to university later on. It's not what we'd have wanted for her, but on the other hand I couldn't live with myself if she blamed us for ruining her chance of a career in dancing.

Valerie, mum to Lauren, 19

Insight

Your main role at this point is to support and counsel, not to intervene, interfere or judge. Your child is at a point in their lives where they must be allowed to trust their own judgement, even if they don't get the outcome they expected. Life is, in a way, a series of stumbling blocks interspersed with smooth paths, and there's nothing wrong with allowing your child to take chances and make decisions for themselves that won't necessarily work out.

Why rules matter

Imagine you could do whatever you pleased whenever you pleased with no recriminations. You might choose to behave pretty much as you do now, but say there were no laws and you could steal, cheat and generally hell-raise at will. How long before you felt directionless, mistrustful of other people, insecure and unhappy, even if you yourself hadn't changed your behaviour? Probably not long. The same is true for children: they thrive on knowing where the boundaries are. If you have a clear set of rules and you instil them in your child, when they choose to push the boundaries they do so knowing what the consequences are likely to be, and they'll have the confidence to try new things, sure that you won't allow them to put themselves in danger or behave inappropriately.

Consistency is also key to maintaining your child's confidence; if the goalposts are constantly moving, this will leave them confused and uncertain of how to behave. If, for example, you're consistent about school night bedtimes, but are usually flexible at the weekends, your child will feel more comfortable about asking for the privilege of an extra late night on a Friday or Saturday if appropriate. But if you suddenly decide you've had enough of your child cutting into your own evening and they must go to bed at the same time every night, weekends included, they'll lose confidence; after all, if this rule can change without warning, so could others – and that will leave them feeling insecure about which boundaries are firm and which aren't. Of course, if you have good reason for shifting bedtimes, such as your child becoming overtired and underperforming at school, or a one-off early start for the whole family next day, this is perfectly acceptable. What is key, though, is that you take the time to explain why the rules are changing rather than simply saying '…because I want you in bed now.' If you don't take the time to do this, they might imagine they've done something wrong that's resulted in the punishment of an earlier bedtime.

> *I hadn't even thought things through from Jayden's point of view when we stopped getting our usual Friday-night takeaway because money was a bit tight. When he questioned me about why we weren't having one, I'd say 'The supermarket had these pizzas on special offer,' or something like that, but of course he didn't equate that with a lack of cash, and I didn't want to worry him that we were going to be poor so I didn't explain any further. By the third weekend he was really despondent and it came out that he thought he was being punished. I was confused until he reminded me that we always used to say 'Have you been a good boy at school this week? OK, then we'll have a takeaway!' Because I didn't bother explaining that we just needed to cut back for a month or two, he'd assumed that he was being bad. I felt terrible that he'd been suffering all that time when a simple explanation was all that was needed.*
>
> Cath, mum to Jayden, eight

The expert view

The Royal College of Psychiatrists offers the following guidelines for setting and managing rules.

Be consistent
If you don't stick to the rules, your children will learn that if they ignore them, you will probably give in.

Give lots of praise
Let your children know when they have done something well and when you are pleased with them. For example, give them a hug, give them a kiss and tell them how great they are. You need to do this straight away.

Planning ahead
It helps if you and your children know the rules in advance for particular situations. Don't make them up as you go along.

Involve your child
Sit down with your children and talk to them about good behaviour. You might be surprised about how much you both agree on.

Be calm
This can be difficult in the heat of the moment, but it does help. Be calm and clear with your commands, for example: 'Please switch off the television' or 'It's bedtime'.

Be clear with your child
For example: 'Please put your toys away' tells children exactly what you expect them to do. Simply telling them to 'be good' does not. If children can't understand you, they can't obey you. Keep it short and simple.

Be realistic
It's no good promising a wonderful reward or dreadful punishment if you're not going to see it through. It's much better to offer small rewards rather than punishments. For example: 'When you've tidied your room, you can have an ice cream.' Don't expect miracles. If your child has only partly tidied their room, praise them for having started.

The importance of your relationship
When times are difficult, it's easy to forget that you can actually have nice times together. You need to plan to have good times. For example, you could play a game, read or cook with them for ten minutes every day.

Insight

Don't beat yourself up if you do make a sudden U-turn on some house rule because it suits you better to do so at the time; just make it clear that this is an exception rather than a complete reversal. It's important you teach your child that there's flexibility within your rules as this means there might be room for negotiation – but only if they can make a good enough case! In the same way, your own best interests count equally alongside theirs, so bending the rules to your own end from time to time is completely acceptable.

THE ROLE OF UNCONDITIONAL LOVE

The basis of great parenting and good discipline is unconditional love – the single biggest factor in building confidence in our children. If we demonstrate it often, both in the way we behave towards them when they fall out of line and by telling them often that we love them no matter what, they'll feel secure and confident to try new things. This doesn't mean condoning misbehaviour or defiance though. You can deliver the message of unconditional love alongside a reminder of the rules and boundaries you expect your child to respect. Giving them the unfailing support of unconditional love is, in any case, more likely to result in desirable behaviour than misbehaviour as your child will naturally aim to live up to your high regard for him. Often, when children are not well aware of their family's unconditional love for them, they will push the boundaries to the limit to test their parents' reactions, and consequently draw their own conclusions – albeit inaccurate – as to how much they are valued.

Why position in the family matters

Recent research by scientists at the University of Oslo supports the idea that birth order can have an influence on intelligence as well as character. Whether your child is the eldest, middle or youngest sibling, or if they are an only child, their position in the family – as well as their own personality – will have an impact on their sense of responsibility and confidence. It's an important consideration when it comes to deciding on the level of responsibility you can reasonably expect – and the level that will make them feel most comfortable and proficient. If you have more than one child, each will each play a role in boosting – or undermining – the confidence of his or her siblings, and you can encourage them to have a positive rather than negative influence (although it would be miraculous if you managed to achieve this within your family at all times, and a bit of healthy adversity is all part of growing up!). As for twins, well most birth order experts believe that each child will tend to take on the characteristics of their joint position within the family.

> **Insight**
> If you do have more than one child, make a point of setting aside a little time to spend one-to-one with each of them on a regular basis. You might not manage it every day, but some quality time once every few days should be achievable. It's important, too, to celebrate each child as an individual by sharing their different interests and praising them for their own separate efforts.

TYPICAL CHARACTERISTICS TO LOOK FOR

Several different research studies, including one conducted at the University of California among more than 2,000 families from six countries found that different birth positions seemed to confer certain personality traits. Here's a rundown of the most typical characteristics and how you can nurture your child's confidence whatever their birth position. The advice applies to all ages and stages.

Your first-born child
First-borns (and only children) have typically been found to display the following characteristics:

- high-achievers
- dominant personalities
- conscientious
- organized
- responsible
- neurotic
- anxious
- conformist.

Your first-born or only child is likely to seek your approval more than their siblings will; they'll thrive on responsibility and your individual time and attention. If they have siblings, you may notice that they're more demanding than when they were an only child. They'll be motivated by praise and a desire to please and can have a tendency to be a bit bossy.

Here are some ways you can encourage your first-born.

▶ Make sure you give them lots of time when they don't have to be in charge or take on too much responsibility.
▶ Don't be afraid to show them that it's OK to fail sometimes as they'll be prone to self-criticism, which in turn can lead to low self-esteem when they can't live up to their own high standards.
▶ Let them regress if they show signs of wanting to. Be free with your kisses and cuddles, and make time to talk to them one-to-one so you can be as in touch as possible with their feelings.
▶ Let them have a say in family decisions that will affect them – they might not particularly enjoy surprises as they like to be in control, so encourage them to plan ahead for any changes that might be coming up.
▶ Let them choose some responsibilities that will be just theirs, but don't let them overload themselves. They won't easily say 'no' and may put themselves under too much pressure, setting themselves up to fail. Giving them manageable tasks will allow them opportunities to bask in your praise.
▶ Encourage them to take a few risks. They'll probably prefer to play safe so they can't fail, but trying new experiences – even if they're not altogether positive straight away – will give them more skills and a broader outlook, which can be very empowering.
▶ Try to make any criticism constructive. So, for instance, instead of saying: 'I knew you'd never finish that homework before dinner – now you've spoilt the rest of the evening for yourself!' say 'Do you think making a homework timetable and sticking to it might make life more manageable?', then help them put this idea into practice. Remember to give at least five times as much praise as you give criticism, and don't worry if this feels contrived at first – it'll soon come naturally!

Your middle-born child
Middle-born children are said to have the following traits:

▶ rebelliousness
▶ free spirits

- impulsiveness
- keen to experiment
- peace-making
- lower-achieving
- less academic.

Sometimes the middle children in a family struggle to find their own place, being neither the first-born nor the baby. This can give them a tendency to indulge in attention-seeking behaviour, and not always positive attention if negative is easier to come by. On the other hand, your middle child is probably eager to keep the peace between other family members and friends, and will have a keen sense of justice – and injustice. They might find it hard to make decisions or form independent opinions, and they'll benefit from being shown the advantages of confident decision-making.

Here are some ways you can encourage your middle child.

- Avoid head-on confrontations, even if this is your child's natural way of communicating. You need to show them that everything can be discussed more constructively if you keep things calm, so tell them you'll listen to them without interruption when they're calmer and then they must listen to you in the same way.
- Let them feel they have some control over things by finding compromises when you have a disagreement.
- Encourage their individuality by letting them have the freedom to explore their own fashion preferences, giving them some say in how their room looks and listening to their ideas, however outlandish, without making fun of them. They might want to take up an unusual hobby or start their own club, so give them your support if they want to strike out on their own.
- Make a point of providing them with some possessions that are just theirs. Middle children tend to inherit clothes, school equipment, toys and other things from their older siblings, and are then expected to pass it all on to younger brothers or sisters.
- Give your middle child plenty of one-to-one attention and make a point of recognizing their achievements. Sometimes the youngest and oldest members of the family will make the greatest demands and are often the most vociferous, so ask your middle child their opinion; encourage them to talk about their feelings; make them feel like an individual.

Your youngest child

Last-borns are said to have the following traits:

▶ geniality
▶ sociability
▶ extroversion
▶ creativity
▶ a fun-loving and funny nature
▶ non-conformity.

Youngest children can play on their position in the family as babies when they want to have their own way (but they can also resent this position when they want to be more grown up). This can mean they're a bit short on taking responsibility – but this is often because they're not given enough in the first place. There's a tendency among families to over-protect and pander to the youngest child because they are the last baby. This can result in spoilt and over-demanding behaviour when taken too far, and youngest children may also grow up to expect too much from future relationships, having been used to getting their own way during their formative years.

Here are some ways you can encourage your youngest.

▶ Appealing to your child's sense of fun and humour can get better results than threatening or punishing him. Show them how to laugh at their own mistakes by laughing at your own – but don't cross the line into making fun of them.
▶ Show them how to see things from other people's points of view. Ask them to find out what different family members want to drink with their dinner, then get out the cups; get them to offer food round when you have visitors; share happy and sad news with them, treading carefully if they're particularly sensitive; be considerate to them – and other people – in return.
▶ Make a special point of praising them for achievements you may otherwise overlook, as you'll have seen them in your older children previously. Don't forget that to them each milestone is new and presents just as much of a challenge as it did to their siblings.
▶ Give them their own specific roles and chores within the home, just as you do with their older brothers and sisters – it's never too early to start. Make them responsible for letting you know when the fruit bowl is running low, for example, or for filling the

pets' water dishes. Don't give him anything too challenging to do though, or you'll be setting them up to fail, and bear in mind you'll probably have to remind them often!

Your only child

Only children share the characteristics of first-borns, but may also have the following traits:

▶ scholarliness
▶ good skills
▶ concentration
▶ precociousness
▶ introspection
▶ good organizational skills.

Only children can also be a little old before their years as they spend more time in exclusively adult company than their peers. Like first-borns (who were, of course, themselves only children for a period of time), they can suffer from a tendency to be self-critical and introspective, and can benefit from being shown how to take themselves a little less seriously.

Here are some ways you can encourage your only child.

▶ Let your child have some independence. There's often a temptation to hover around an only child, especially if you imagine they're lonely without siblings to play with. They are likely to have a fertile imagination and be happy to spend time in their own company sometimes, as long as you're there to play with them sometimes when they do want company.
▶ Avoid being over-protective. Your child needs to be able to stand on their own two feet and could become anxious when left to their own devices if they haven't been encouraged to try new experiences. Let them take small risks while telling them you're there for them all the way.
▶ Be careful not to over-indulge your child. They don't need an endless supply of material things to entertain them or make them feel loved. The best gift you can give them is your attention and lots of love and hugs.
▶ Only children can become over-involved in adult concerns, especially as they have no siblings to distract them, so agree with your partner that you'll try to keep any conversations that could make your child anxious for after they have gone to bed.

- Join them up to social groups and after-school clubs, and get them involved with other children to give them lots of opportunities for making friends and spending time with people their own age. Encourage them to bring friends home and have sleepovers. It will help if you make friends with some of their peers' parents too.
- Encourage them to take turns and share – traits which may not come as easily to an only child as they might to children who have to share with siblings. Only children can be a bit competitive, so play games that need co-operation, and let them wait a minute or two sometimes when they're looking for your attention, perhaps when you're on the phone or watching the end of a favourite television programme.

Celebrity birth order

Can you recognize any of the traits described above in these famous people?

- First-borns: Winston Churchill; Prince Charles; Oprah Winfrey; David Attenborough; Rudyard Kipling; George W Bush; Bill Clinton; Hillary Clinton; J K Rowling.
- Middle-borns: Prince Andrew; Ricky Gervais; Dawn French; Julia Roberts; Princess Diana; Glenn Close; Richard Nixon; Donald Trump; Ted Kennedy.
- Last-borns: Chris Evans; Joely Richardson; George Michael; Jim Carrey; Steve Martin; Billy Crystal; Danny DeVito; Goldie Hawn; Prince Edward.
- Only children: Robin Williams; Cary Grant; Isaac Newton; Indira Ghandi; Joseph Stalin; Franklin D Roosevelt; Jean Paul Sartre; Brooke Shields; Frank Sinatra; Tiger Woods.

Giving your child appropriate responsibilities

You can help boost your child's confidence by giving them age-appropriate responsibilities from toddlerhood onwards. The more they manage to do independently, the more their self-esteem will blossom and the more willing they'll be to try something else, so make sure whatever you do assign to them is within their grasp. Here are some ideas for responsibilities you could give them at different ages and stages:

Age of child	Responsibility
3–4	Choosing a toy for bedtime Putting their shoes away Helping to carry non-breakables to and from the dinner table Handing out napkins Choosing a bedtime storybook Rinsing their own toothbrush Turning the television off
5–6	Finding and handing you grocery items in the supermarket Helping to pair up washed socks Finding the cutlery for dinner Hanging their own coat on a low peg Washing themselves in the bath/shower Hanging up their own school uniform
7–8	Helping to load and unload the dishwasher Helping to pack the shopping in the supermarket Packing their own schoolbag Having a wash and brushing their teeth morning and night Helping out with the care of younger siblings
9–10	Keeping account of their own pocket money Making their own bed Setting aside time for their homework, and starting to work independently Venturing out to the local shop alone (as long as they are road-safety aware) Going out for a bike ride with friends (if your neighbourhood is suitable) Helping out with the care of younger siblings
11–13	Taking on some regular household chores, such as cleaning the bathroom/vacuuming Making their own snacks Making you a cup of tea

Age of child	Responsibility
	Going out with friends and making their own travel arrangements
	Managing their own money when out
	Keeping tabs on their mobile phone credit
	Scheduling their homework and spending enough time on it
14+	Babysitting younger siblings
	Finding ways of earning extra pocket money (e.g. delivering free newspapers)
	Getting themselves off to school if you and your partner both work
	Organizing and taking younger siblings to school
	Making their own breakfast
	Being able to cook simple meals
	Helping more around the house (within reason if they have a lot of homework or revision)
	Running a bank account with a debit card (although you may need to help at first)

Insight

Some children are ready for greater responsibility younger – or older – than others, so let your child set the pace. The recommendations outlined above are just that and not set in stone. Every child is an individual and must be allowed to develop at their own rate without feeling pressurized either by family or peers.

Teach your child to take pride in their work

As your child grows, more will be expected of them at school and by any extra-curricular teachers. One way you can help teach them to take pride in their work is by setting an example. There's a fine balance between being slapdash and being a perfectionist, and if you naturally fall into either camp it'll take a bit of focus on your part to either raise or drop your standards to whatever level you expect of your child. Of course, you can't apply this to everything you do; some things just need more attention to detail than others, and this is another good lesson for your child to learn. There'll be occasions, too, when you're just too pushed to do a proper job: you might have five minutes to bring the washing in from the line, for instance, but no extra time to fold or pair it up; you might be able to stack the dishes after dinner, but have to wait until after the children are in bed before you can tackle the washing up. That's not important. But if you're wrapping a special present, laying the table for guests or helping your child with their homework, let them see you giving the job your full attention and showing pleasure in the result.

Your child will have a sense of pride in their work if you display it around the home too: not everything they produce has to be a masterpiece, but anything they've really tried hard at is worthy of showing off on their behalf. If they do a particularly good drawing or piece of handwriting, maybe you could laminate it to give it a longer display life.

Talk to your child about their favourite idols; how do they imagine they became so successful? Would that premier league footballer have been bought by the team without getting to peak fitness and building up a fantastic skill set? What about their favourite rock band? Could they all play so well as a group without lots of practice sessions? Explain that all successful people take great pride in their work and usually devote a lot of time to maintaining or improving their standards. OK, so they may never achieve fame or great fortune, but the way to make progress in all walks of life is to apply themselves and persevere.

If your child is struggling in any of their school subjects, it's important to support them by contacting their teacher so you can work out how to put a plan of action together for them. It might involve you doing extra work at home with them; perhaps there's a lunchtime drop-in session they could go to sometimes; maybe their teacher can bring them to the front of the classroom where she can keep a closer eye on their progress. Don't worry that by highlighting their difficulty you'll have undermined their confidence – actually the reverse is true. Showing them that you understand the problem and feel sure they can improve will bolster their self-esteem and, as long as the issue is approached sympathetically, they'll feel that they can get there in the end. There's nothing more disempowering than being out of your depth while your peers are all managing beautifully, and once they've got the extra support and start making progress, that'll give them a huge confidence boost too.

10 THINGS TO REMEMBER

1 Encourage team play within the family – not just when you're playing games, but by co-operating with each other in running the home.

2 Give your child age-appropriate responsibilities, and review regularly what they're capable of.

3 Broaden their social life so they get to play with children of a variety of ages – boys as well as girls – and interact with other adults.

4 Increase their independence gradually to boost their self-esteem.

5 Use positive affirmations and humour rather than warnings to encourage good behaviour in your child.

6 Support your child with their homework. Sit alongside and be on hand if they need help (but don't be tempted to do it for them!).

7 Remember that respect is a two-way thing, so give your child as much respect as you expect to get back.

8 Set clear rules and boundaries so your child feels safe and secure.

9 Reinforce your unconditional love by telling your child that although you may not always approve of their actions or choices you will always love them.

10 Acknowledge the birth position of your child – and each of their siblings – and make efforts to bring out and nurture their individuality.

4

....

Empowering with life skills

In this chapter you will learn:
- *how learning new skills builds confidence*
- *which skills you can teach your child*
- *how to teach your child without taking over*
- *about building body confidence.*

New skills, new confidence

We all feel great about ourselves when we begin to master a new skill, whatever it might be. With encouragement and practice we grow in proficiency, and our self-esteem grows in the same measure. There are many opportunities to teach your child new skills – some mundane, others more challenging – from babyhood right through to adulthood, from practical to intellectual and emotional.

Until babies reach an age where they can start to make a little sense of the world around them, other people are their only source of enlightenment, and right from day one you'll have been teaching your baby new skills, whether you're aware of it or not. Learning happens very rapidly from birth throughout childhood, with the fastest rate happening between birth and age seven. In the late 1990s, developmental psychologists in the US discovered that by the time children reach age three, their brains are twice as active as adults' brains, so by this stage they've already have acquired an enormous amount of information and are keen to experiment with their knowledge.

Later on, during the school years, it will help if you can identify what sort of learner your child is. The most commonly used system in schools, widely promoted by the Department for Education in the UK, is the VAK classification system, which divides children into visual, auditory or kinaesthetic (also known as active) learners: those who like to look, those who like to listen and those who learn best through hands-on experience.

Your child may show a preference for one learning style but they may also manage well with others, or they may have no great preference. Once you've identified your child's style, you can adapt the way you teach them at home. You can find out about their style from the school if it has run the VAK tests, or you can find free tests online. In any case, you'll probably be able to get a fair idea yourself by trial and error, for example by using different techniques to teach your child if they don't seem to be getting along with the first you try.

> **Insight**
>
> If your child has a marked preference, playing to their particular learning style will boost their confidence no end. If you're tapping into their style, they'll acquire skills and information more quickly and assimilate it more efficiently, whereas using an approach they don't get on with so well can give them the wrong impression that they just can't do what it is you're trying to show them.

Skills you can teach your child

The same as when you're giving your child responsibility, their age and general ability should dictate which skills you can introduce or encourage. Here are some examples of the sorts of practical, intellectual and emotional things you can teach your child at each age and stage.

YOUR BABY

Your baby will learn certain skills as a matter of course through normal development, but you can certainly enhance their learning and even introduce new ideas from babyhood.

Practical skills
- ▶ Once your baby can sit unsupported, scatter a few of their favourite toys just out of their reach and watch them stretch to grab them. Even at this stage they'll be chuffed with their own achievement.
- ▶ Once they can cruise (get around in a standing position, holding on to furniture for support), encourage them to stretch across safe surfaces to reach their toys.

▶ Give them plenty of finger foods (from around seven months) so they can hone their finger-and-thumb pincer grip. At first they might chuck more food about than they eat, though, so it's best only to give them finger foods once they've already eaten something or they may become frustrated: just after a small milk feed or halfway through a bowl of purée is a good idea.

Intellectual skills
▶ Pull exaggerated faces at your young baby (happy, not scary!) and watch them mimic you. Studies by US psychologists Andrew N Meltzoff and M Keith Moore during the 1970s and 1980s suggested that even newborns had an inbuilt response that allowed them to mimic an adult sticking their tongue out. Their studies showed that babies recognized pictures of adults who had previously stuck out their tongues at them, and responded by sticking their own tongues out, but didn't react when shown pictures of adults who hadn't stuck their tongues out. Many parents find that their newborn will mimic making an 'O' shape with their lips in response to them doing it first. It seems this is instinctive at this stage, because it's not until around four months that babies are really able to learn to copy other facial expressions and physical gestures.
▶ Read to your baby often. They'll soon pick up the gist from your tone of voice, as well as learning that stories progress on the page from left to right and top to bottom, with words having connections with the corresponding pictures. If you point at pictures as you describe them – and look at the same books often – you'll notice that eventually your older baby will point to objects you name in the pictures.
▶ When they are in her highchair after eating, give them a wooden spoon and an upturned plastic bowl and encourage them to beat out a simple rhythm. This will help develop hand-eye coordination as well as building their strength.
▶ Teach your baby to use sign language. Research has shown that babies who can sign have fewer tantrums during that difficult period when they understand more language than they can actually articulate. Professor Karen Pine from the University of Hertfordshire, who led one study, said: 'We have found that encouraging mothers to use simple hand gestures with their infants can have linguistic and wider non-linguistic benefits for

infants.' You can find different courses and local groups online, but you can also try devising your own language. If, for instance, you consistently use a certain gesture when you say 'hungry' to your baby, they'll quickly use the same gesture to tell you when they want food. The same applies to all the commonest requirements: 'drink'; 'tired'; 'hurts'; 'cuddle'; 'carry'; 'play' and so on.

I didn't realize just how much a baby under a year old could learn and was amazed when at ten months Lottie was able to anticipate me clapping along to her baby music CD after I'd only done it a couple of times. She waved her own hands around and was bobbing up and down to the rhythm! She seems much more caring than I thought babies her age were capable of too, really burying her head in my neck and hugging me whenever I pick her up. It's all so sweet!

Carrie, mum to Lottie, 11 months

Emotional skills

▶ You can begin to teach your baby empathy from very early on by giving them (newborn-safe) cuddly toys to cherish. Cuddle their teddy, then hand it to them to cuddle; say 'Aaah, poor Teddy!' when they throw him to the floor, then pick him up and comfort him. Similarly, when your baby is upset, use a deliberately comforting tone of voice to soothe them – this will probably come naturally. And when you're watching cartoons or other children's television programmes together, laugh at the funny parts, empathize with the sadder bits and give them a lovely hug during the heart-warming scenes.

▶ Let your baby see you caring for the family's pets: chat to them rather than just feeding and watering them; stroke and play with them in front of your child whenever you get a chance and encourage your child to do the same.

Insight

It's easy to think that babies have little in the way of understanding or imagination, but there's so much more going on in their heads than we're aware of that it's definitely worth communicating new ideas, holding conversations with your baby and stimulating their senses from very early on – as long as you also recognize when they're becoming over-stimulated and needs some downtime.

Toddlers gain knowledge and skills at a fantastic rate, so it's a great time to tap in to all this learning potential. Never has the analogy 'soaking up information like a sponge' been more accurately applied than to this age group. Your toddler may be more capable than you imagine, and as long as you don't overload them with responsibility or give them tasks they're likely to fail at – or that present some sort of danger – you may be surprised by how much they can actually do.

Practical skills

▶ Provide them with their own mini gardening set and a couple of fast-growing plants, such as cress, nasturtiums or beans, to care for. Of course, you'll have to help them, but they'll probably be happy to pull out any small weeds around the plants and give them a gentle watering. Take regular photos of their plants so they can look back on their progress.

▶ Give your child a toddler cutlery set: a knife, fork and spoon, not just spoon and fork. Show them how to hold them, and get them to practise when they're not too hungry – perhaps halfway through a meal at first – that way they won't be too frustrated if things fall off their cutlery or if they miss their mouth (and they will!). Plan for some mess by putting down a plastic sheet or some towels, encourage every attempt and don't make a fuss if they drop food on the floor or resort to using fingers. This is all part of the process.

▶ If you haven't yet taken your child swimming, enrol them in some lessons as soon as possible. They'll gain most confidence from learning with other children of the same age and ability. Never try to teach your child to swim by dropping them into a pool and letting them rely on their instincts – this can trigger a life-long fear of water.

▶ Let them take a toy shopping trolley or wheelie basket to the shops with you and bring some of the shopping home. It'll make them feel responsible and grown-up, as well as encouraging coordination and balance.

▶ Teach them what to do if they find themselves separated from you while you're out together. Tell them who is safest to approach, like police officers, people working on the tills in shops, and mums with children. Teach them to say 'I'm lost' and to give their name and yours. (Some parents sew their mobile phone numbers into their children's clothing or coat pockets; this might work for you, too, as long as your child knows it's there!) Practise this new skill often through role-play – it's a really important one.

Intellectual skills

▶ Start teaching your child the alphabet from age two or so. They probably won't memorize the whole thing for some time yet, but it's good to get the practice in early. Don't worry about cross-over with any formal teaching at this stage – you're only helping them recognize a few letters, which should also spark an interest in reading later on. Point out their initial when you see it out and about on posters, hoardings and in shops, sounding it rather than naming the letter: so say 'Look, "puh" for Polly' rather than 'Look, "pee" for Polly'. This is called phonetic pronunciation. Get hold of a good alphabet-based book and read it with them often; buy a set of magnetic alphabet pieces and play with them on the front of the fridge.

▶ You can introduce some number work now, too. Show your child how to count toys into a basket; sing a number song using your fingers to show them how many each number stands for; once they can count to five, use fruit, building bricks or any other simple shapes to show them how $1 + 1 = 2$, $2 + 2 = 4$ or $4 + 1 = 5$; count your way up and down stairs, letting them say the numbers on their own if they know them.

▶ Give them a tape measure and encourage them to measure things. It doesn't matter that they don't understand the actual measurements or that they're accurate; it'll show them numbers appearing in sequence and help to teach the concept that they can represent different measurements.

▶ Introduce them to a musical keyboard. It shows numeric progressions as the notes go up one step at a time; your child might not grasp this concept at first but the abstract will get into their brain in any case.

Jamie has really got into looking for his initial. In fact, it took me a while to make the connection that he'd seen it. We've got a shop called Jessops in town and he recently started pointing at the shop going 'Jamie, Jamie!'. I was puzzled the first once or twice, but eventually I realized it was the 'J' he'd recognized. Aren't children amazing?

Alicia, mum to Jamie, two and a half, and Aimee, six months

Emotional skills

▶ All toddlers will have tantrums from time to time – it's their way of expressing frustration. An important skill to teach your toddler is how to calm themselves. You can do this by example (although it may well take you some practice yourself and won't be appropriate in every social situation): when they go into a tantrum, do your best to remain calm; slow your breathing; lower your voice; move them to a safe space and hold them firmly by the upper arms if you can; look into their eyes and let them assimilate the rhythm of your breathing and your calm behaviour. Once the tantrum subsides, give them a close cuddle and talk to them in a soothing tone of voice. This technique proves to your child that they can't rattle you by throwing a tantrum, and helps them to allow things to return to normal more quickly.

▶ Boost your child's emotional development by spending lots of one-to-one time with them. Ask them questions you know they'll be confident in answering; this will boost their self-esteem no end and let them ask you lots of questions, too. Showing that you're prepared to listen and take time to explain things to them will make them feel valued and increase their self-esteem.

▶ Teach your child that praise is a two-way thing by practising it around them and praising and appreciating them. Remember to try to balance any criticism with five lots of praise, even if it's only 'Thank you for helping' or 'You've done that really well.' Encourage them to say 'please' and 'thank you' at home as well as elsewhere so that it becomes a natural part of their language. Let them hear you praising and appreciating your partner, other siblings and visitors to your home too.

Insight

You can help your child gain emotional intelligence by encouraging them to talk to other people and getting them to think about what the other people are telling them. Get family and friends to ask them open questions that need more than a one-word answer, like 'What was the best bit of your day today?' rather than 'Have you had a lovely day?' They might not be able to articulate much yet, but it's still worth getting them into the habit of two-way conversation.

YOUR YOUNG CHILD

Rising fives and primary-age schoolchildren are still learning rapidly and will be keen to take on more responsibilities and prove themselves with their new skills. It's important to stretch them a bit with age-appropriate challenges that are within their own ability levels.

Practical skills

▶ Let your child help you with the laundry. They can sort it into coloureds and whites or underwear and outerwear. Ask them to fetch the basket when the washing finishes and help you pull it out of the machine. They can bring the pegs and – with the help of a step-up – help hang the washing out, then help bring it in and fold it when it's dry.

▶ Show them how to make themselves a healthy snack. It could be a sandwich (but make sure first that the butter or spread is soft enough to use easily); a bowl of soft fruits, chopped with a bluntish knife (with your supervision); a milkshake or smoothie (again, with your supervision) or a homemade ice lolly (you can buy moulds and kits inexpensively from supermarkets and homeware departments).

▶ Make them responsible for checking their own school supplies. Are their pencils all sharpened? Do their felt-tipped pens still work? Do they have a working glue stick? Is everything labelled? Give them a hug and some words of praise whenever they remember to check it all without being reminded.

▶ Give them their own list of regular chores to do. They could be responsible for tidying away everyone's shoes; wiping around the bathroom basin; helping to unstack the dishwasher; drying up unbreakables or any other task you think they'll manage well.

▶ Let them brush their own hair morning and evening. You could get them to do their teeth as well, but according to NHS guidelines they'll need you to finish the job off properly for them until they're around age seven as they won't have the dexterity to reach all the hard-to-get-to areas before then.

Intellectual skills

▶ Make up stories with your child. You create the opening paragraph, and then encourage them to take the story up; take it in turns to add bits as you go along, letting them take the lead. Get them to jot down key words and draw simple pictures on pieces of card. You can use these as prompts when you tell your story to the rest of the family.

▶ Play simple spelling games. Write some common words on pieces of card and let your child memorize them (no more than five or so at a time). Then give them cards with the same words on them, but with one or two letters missing, and get them to fill in the blanks. You can find interactive spelling games online, too, or play family games like Junior Scrabble and Boggle Junior.

▶ Encourage your child to read every day. You can either read with them or to them, or you can encourage them to read to you (they'll probably get this as daily homework in any case). Avoid the temptation to jump straight in if they're a bit stuck on a word; get them to sound it out or give them a clue as to what the word might be. If they're getting very frustrated, though, do tell them or they'll lose the confidence to continue. It's a great idea to join the local library and get your child their own card at this stage.

▶ Engage them in conversation at mealtimes. Get them thinking about things and coming up with their own opinions and ideas. You can prompt them with open questions that can't simply be answered 'yes' or 'no'.

▶ Encourage them to take up a musical instrument. If they're at school you might be offered lessons free of charge or at a subsidized rate or, if you can play yourself, perhaps you could get them started. Otherwise, ask around for recommendations of local teachers. Don't choose anything too tricky at first, and bear in mind that if you choose an instrument that comes in different sizes, such as a violin, you may have quite a lot of outlay as they progress.

None of us is really musical in our family, but when Ollie was offered free violin lessons at school, he seemed quite keen. He's really taken to it, so I'm not too bothered that he has to miss a classroom lesson to go to his violin lesson once a week. They're talking about putting him in for Grade I and he's only been learning about 10 months. They do say there's a link between music and maths, and I've noticed that his number work is improving too, although that could be a coincidence. Either way, it's a good result!

Arianne, mum to Ollie, seven

Emotional skills

▶ It's often once children are established at school that they really start to understand empathy as an emotion. If they come home with tales of upsets, try to get them to see things from all points of view and tell you how they think each person might have been feeling. It will help them to take a step back when they're involved in any spats themselves.

▶ Teach your child conflict resolution skills – these will prove invaluable as they go through life, even from this young age. Encourage them to be the peacemaker in squabbles with family and friends. You can practise this in the home if they have younger siblings or similar-age cousins or neighbours. Explain that everyone is entitled to an opinion, and that most minor arguments aren't worth wasting time on if everyone involved can be persuaded to make peace with each other. Tell them, too, that you don't necessarily have to apologize to make things better if you don't feel you were to blame: often it helps just to say 'I'm sorry you were upset'. The difference is subtle, but important.

▶ The world outside home can be a confusing place to grow up in, so set aside time to chat to your child each day and see if you can find out how they're feeling about things. You may be able to help them unravel any mixed-up feelings, or it might be enough just to listen. Either way you'll be teaching them the importance of recognizing other people's feelings and just being there for them. Give them a lovely close cuddle whenever they're feeling vulnerable (or any other time it seems welcome!).

▶ Teach them to appreciate other people's differences. Not everyone has the same skin colour, beliefs, social background, family customs or culture. Some people don't speak English as a first language; others may wear special clothing in line with their faith; some people are disabled, mentally or physically. Talk to them about how every person is of equal value, and explain that while it's OK to compare them with themselves, it isn't right to make a judgement.

Insight

Getting your child to help prepare their own food, where appropriate, can be very helpful if they're a faddy eater. Children often take a great enough pride in their own efforts to want to try them and for you to try them too, so you may have to stomach some rather weird concoctions if they decide to invent their own recipes. The important thing is to let them have free rein (with ingredients carefully selected by you!) to experiment.

YOUR TWEENIE

At this age, your child's likely to be champing at the bit to get more freedom and do most things for themselves. The only thing to watch out for is that you don't get sucked in to believing they're capable of more than they're really mature enough to handle. But it's a good time to build on and expand their skills base.

Practical skills

▶ Show them how to put a packed lunch together for school. OK, they might not get round to doing it every night, but it'll be a good thing if they can manage to get a healthy balance whenever they do make their own lunch. Keep a good supply of unrefined carbs, pieces of fruit, low-fat dairy products and other healthy snacks in the house so they'll have plenty of choice available.

▶ Let them loose with the iron. It may be a skill you've been putting off teaching them because of the risk of burns, but they've got the dexterity and it's time to help them tackle some everyday potential dangers now. Make sure you encourage your son, as well as your daughter, to iron – there's no reason for the chore to stay in the female domain and you'll be doing any future girlfriends/ daughter-in-law a huge favour if you domesticate your son.

▶ Teach them how to brew the perfect cuppa – for you, if not for themselves. It'll probably be a novelty at first, but there's no reason why one of their daily contributions to the home shouldn't be to make at least one round of tea.

▶ Show them how to do some basic sewing. It doesn't have to be cross-stitch – in fact sewing on a button is a more useful skill at this stage. Choose a fairly thick needle with a large eye to start with and let them practise on some old clothes.

Intellectual skills

▶ The ante will be well and truly upped in terms of study, homework and revision once your child reaches high school, so now's the time to instil good habits. Help them set up a quiet study area if you can manage the space. Perhaps you could sacrifice a toy cupboard for a small desk and chair set, or maybe you have an under-stairs area that could house a computer set-up. Make sure you consult with your child so they feel properly involved and will enjoy using their new facilities. Put up a whiteboard weekly planner where they can write down which homework is due in when, then rub each assignment off as they complete it.

▶ Let your child take on responsibilities such as uploading and downloading family photos from digital cameras. Practising their computer skills will stand them in good stead as well as giving them a grown-up role.

▶ Challenge your child to read more. You could perhaps agree to read the same book, then compare notes – like in your own mini book club. If they're not keen to do this with you, suggest they put the idea to a friend. (At this stage it really doesn't matter what they're reading, as long as it's age-appropriate; the important thing is to encourage them to read. You can always make sure you suggest some cool titles based around their own interests.)

▶ If you're into word games like crosswords, or number puzzles like Sudoku, buy a book of easy puzzles and show your child how they're done. Cryptic puzzles are really good for the development of lateral thinking – another great skill for high school work, when they'll be expected to start thinking outside the box.

▶ Get them interested in the news. CBBC's *Newsround* is a great television programme to start with, and there's a corresponding website too. You could also take out a subscription to a children's newspaper online. Encourage them to listen to some of the hourly news bulletins on their favourite radio station – they only last about three minutes, so it shouldn't be too much of a challenge. Try to get them to discuss at least one news story per day with another member of the family, and encourage them to express their own view. It's really important not to make fun of them though, so even if they do come to a rather surprising conclusion or make a snap judgement about something, just say 'It's an interesting viewpoint. Have you thought about it this way?'

Emotional skills

▶ It's a time of great emotional upheaval for many children, especially once they become pre-pubescent and are at the mercy of their hormones. It's also another opportunity for you to suggest to your child strategies for handling themselves that'll stand them in good stead generally. What's important is that you first have a conversation about the effect on mood that hormones can have, and how this might affect them. Reassure them that it's perfectly normal to feel weepy, irritable or plain angry with no rational cause at certain times, then give them some ideas for coping (such as counting to ten and taking deep breaths; having a warm bath and an early night; asking you for a comforting cuddle; punching a pillow; going for a run into an open space and practising some primal screaming – whatever works!). Knowing that you understand and will be supportive (with the caveat that, try as you might, you may just crack yourself because you're only human!) will gain their trust in you.

▶ Share some slightly more adult humour (within reason) with your child; they'll really appreciate being let in on the joke and are less likely to keep cracking inappropriate gags and trying to shock you if you treat them as more mature.

▶ See if they'd like to take on responsibility for other children in some supervised capacity. This can be simple to organize if they already have some out-of-school interests and are fairly mature. Could they, for instance, babysit a neighbour's child – or their younger siblings? Could they help out at Brownies/Scouts or help coach the beginners at the local swimming club? Would their middle school appreciate help with school productions in the evenings or weekends? Perhaps there's some voluntary work they could get involved with? It'll all be great training for any leadership courses they take later on, too.

▶ Encourage your child to keep in touch with you about how they're getting on at school. Once they reach high school and you lose that interaction with other parents and staff, children often regard their day as somehow private. (Ever tried asking a high schooler what they did at school and got the answer 'Don't know', 'Can't remember' or – worst of all – 'Nothing'? Point made!) A good technique for opening up discussion is to reminisce about your own early high school days. You could say 'Got any nicknames for your teachers yet? We had some really funny ones for ours' or something similar they'll relate to. A light-hearted conversation can sometimes give rise to a more serious exchange.

I've found that a great place to chat is in the car when you don't have to make eye contact. Sometimes children will open up about things they wouldn't otherwise want to have an earnest conversation about. It's almost as if the conversation is somehow off the record because you're not looking at each other. It's worked a treat with both my boys.

Christianna, mum to Joshua, 11, and Rhys, nine

Insight

A lot will be expected of your child at high school, so it's not too soon
to boost their confidence with more skills. They'll benefit not only from
organizational skills, but also social ones – and these can be quite complex
at this age, especially as children reach different levels of maturity at different
stages. Try to talk about situations that make them feel uneasy, awkward or
embarrassed and give them some ways to overcome them.

YOUR TEEN

Teenagers get a pretty bad press generally these days – often unfairly.
There's no need to dread the teen years though – there are a few key
ways you can maintain your teen's trust as well as enjoying mutual
respect. The first stumbling block to avoid is the urge to become your
child's best mate. Teenagers want a very separate identity from their
parents', so try not to dress similarly, don't offer to swap clothes and
accessories – let your teen take the lead on this – and do encourage
your child to follow their own fashion instincts as far as is reasonable.

Another urge to avoid is trying to interfere in your child's private life,
which – up to a point – should remain private. It's hard, in this digital
age, to give free rein with social networking sites, mobile phones and
so on, and you'll need to insist on some transparency when your child
is online, but don't become so strict in other areas that your child
looks for ways to escape your scrutiny and deliberately go against
the rules. As long as you review the boundaries regularly and update
them where appropriate so that your child has a level of freedom
you're both happy with, your relationship has a good chance of
thriving and your teen is less likely to feel the need to stage a serious
rebellion. You may have to accept, though, that some degree of
anarchy is to be expected. This is a stage where plenty of teenagers
feel they can right all the world's wrongs, and where they tend to
adopt the belief that they know everything. They may take on some
pretty extreme political views, too. All of this is part of healthy
development and shows that your child has the confidence to
experiment with ideas as well as fashion styles.

Practical skills

▶ Start teaching your child some basic cooking skills. Get them
  involved with preparing the evening meal with you, or helping
  you to cook breakfast at the weekends. Once you're sure they
  can manage safely, let them choose what they'd most like to

have a go at, provide them with the right utensils and ingredients and let them get on with it. Be ready to step in if they need help, but there's no need to hover at their shoulder unless they ask you to stay around. If they enjoy cooking, gradually expand their repertoire so that they can competently make themselves something to eat without being reliant on you.

▶ Show your child how to replace a fuse, change a light bulb and reset a trip switch safely. This will stand them in good stead for times when they might find themselves home alone. They'll probably feel empowered by knowing they can do some minor fixes around the house.

▶ If they haven't already got into bed-changing, now's the time to teach them. You could show them how to do their own laundry too, if they're willing. Don't overload them with too many chores and responsibilities though, as they'll probably have plenty of school work to focus on. On the other hand, it's reasonable to expect them to earn their pocket money at this stage.

▶ When they're at the stage where they come and go as they please, make sure they know how to lock the house up securely, and show them how to use the house alarm if you have one. (It's a good idea to leave a spare house key with a trusted neighbour as teenagers can be easily distracted and have a tendency to forget or lose theirs.)

▶ Familiarize your child with local transport links and, if there's an electronic card system (such as Oyster) in your area, get them used to using their own. Show them how to read a timetable; how to navigate the Underground or subway; which bus routes go where; and where they can catch a tram. Work out an alternative routes for when something gets cancelled or delayed.

Intellectual skills

▶ Develop your child's interest and aptitude for school subjects by doing things together that back up the learning: a trip to a museum; a day at an art gallery; a look around a stately home of the period in history they're learning about; renting a World War II DVD; reading a book together that's centred on a geographical place they're studying – all these activities will enhance their studies and help bring the subject to life for them. Get them to bring a friend along if it makes the outing more appealing.

- ▶ Offer them appropriate opportunities to make decisions for themselves, even if they turn out to be mistakes. Often the best way teenagers learn about life is by trial and error, and each time they have to find things out for themselves, their knowledge base and confidence will increase.
- ▶ Encourage your child to challenge accepted wisdom and formulate their own opinions.
- ▶ Help your child develop their memory. They can use a brain-training programme on a handheld game, find online memory games or play pairs using a pack of cards. Teach them how to use mnemonics (such as Rhythm Helps Your Two Hips Move as an aid to spelling 'rhythm' or My Very Easy Method Just Speeds Up Naming Planets for remembering the order of the planets) to remember lists of things, or to create a story in their head to prompt them.
- ▶ Point out to your child the areas of her school subjects that have an overlap: geography, science and music all have mathematical elements; English is carried over into all subjects that require essays and discourse. If they have a weakness in one area, consider getting them extra tuition to boost their confidence in that subject and its overlap areas.

Emotional skills
- ▶ Whether or not you relish the idea, now is the time – if you haven't already approached the subject – to talk to your child about relationships and sex. Chat about how meaningful relationships always involve emotional attachment and explain that, although sex may soon become very appealing in its own right, they need to gain emotional maturity before they're ready to embark on a sexual relationship. Give them some strategies for avoiding having sex until they're ready: they'll probably come under lots of peer pressure and may feel stupid if they don't go along with it, but if they're armed with some excuses, they'll avoid the awful possibility of an unwanted pregnancy or sexually transmitted infection, as well as having treated something very special and serious far too lightly. If they're at a party and under pressure they could make their excuses and leave early or say that they're waiting until they can be alone with someone. If their friends are all boasting about having had sex, they could always act cool and tell a white lie saying they're tried it already and what's the big deal?

▶ Discuss their attitude to the opposite sex and their own; talk about the confusing, ambivalent feelings teenagers may have about their sexuality and how it's not unusual to develop a crush on someone of the same gender for a while; impress on them the importance of respecting their body and others people's, as well as the importance of maintaining personal privacy. Explain that giving away your virginity may seem like an important rite of passage as a teenager, but that ideally it should be something that happens within a loving relationship. Make sure they know that you're open to more discussion and will clarify anything they want you to – but don't be surprised if they don't take you up on your offer!

▶ If, on the other hand, you both feel they're ready for a sexual relationship – or if you think they're likely to start one regardless of your advice – it might be best to prepare them physically by discussing and arranging contraception, preferably in consultation with their GP. Condoms should be a must in all situations until they're in a permanent relationship, because of the risk of sexually transmitted infections (STIs). According to the Health Protection Agency (HPA), chlamydia is currently the most common sexually transmitted infection diagnosed and treated in the UK, and the highest rates are seen in the under-25 age group. The infection, which usually shows no symptoms, can cause infertility among other health problems.

▶ Talk to your child about drugs and alcohol and the inherent dangers. Don't imagine that by opening up the discussion you'll somehow awaken their interest in them; they're going to come into contact with them and face temptation whether you like it or not. You *must* have the conversation and keep the dialogue going. You'll need to find strategies you can give them for resisting peer pressure, such as excuses like 'No, I can't have a drink, I've got an important swimming trial tomorrow' or 'My family is anti-drugs and they'd kill me if they found out, so no thanks' or simply walking away. They could even just say 'Not my thing, thanks' or something equally non-committal. Tell them that drugs and alcohol make teens more prone to dangerous accidents, and that you can never trust the quality or content of drugs or know exactly how you will respond to them. Explain that drugs have poisoned and killed plenty of young people their age and that their life is too precious to take these chances. Warn them that serious addiction could land them in prison, make them bankrupt and unemployable, disable or kill them.

▶ Try to provide your child with other adult role models than you as parents. Sometimes they may need to refer to someone outside of the immediate family, or they may feel more comfortable discussing certain issues with someone slightly removed. Don't take offence at this: they're only one development stage away from becoming an adult and is just beginning the breakaway process, which is encouragingly normal. Beware of adults who ask them to keep secrets though. Keeping your child's confidence is one thing, but swearing them to secrecy is quite another.

▶ Make your child aware of the dangers of internet use. Talk about 'grooming' (where predatory adults pose as peers to vulnerable children to gain their confidence, and then arrange to meet, usually with a view to sexual abuse). Give your child a checklist of behaviours of other adults towards them that should ring alarm bells. Is anyone invading their personal space regularly? Do they feel they're being touched inappropriately (however apparently innocuously, if it doesn't feel right, it probably isn't)? Caution them never to hand over their personal details, either online or in person, without checking with you or another trusted adult first.

Lucy has always been emotionally quite young for her age and very trusting of everyone – known or otherwise. I'm so glad I had the conversation about potentially dangerous adults with her, as she was so shocked and surprised that I could see she may have been very vulnerable to inappropriate approaches or worse. I had to suppress my natural urge to protect her from unpleasant information and just get on with it, even though I knew she'd find it upsetting. It's a shame to have to arouse suspicion in such a trusting child, but better she has the knowledge now than is left to learn from some awful experience.

Julie, mum to Lucy, 13

Teaching without taking over

Are you the sort of parent who would rather jump in and do things for your child than stand by and let them have a good go at it themselves first? It can be very frustrating to watch a child struggling with something without interfering – especially when it's blindingly simple to an adult – but it'll be far more encouraging for your child if you can resist the urge. Give yourselves plenty of time when you're going to coach your child in some new skill; there's nothing worse than feeling pressurized – you or them – when what's really required is a relaxed approach and plenty of patience. Explain exactly what you're going to show them, get all the necessary equipment together, then give them one simple step to do at a time. Depending on what it is you're teaching them, you may both feel more comfortable if you work alongside them at something else so that they don't feel you're watching them like a hawk.

You'll have to accept that some of the skills you teach your child will involve a small degree of risk, whether it's tackling a large climbing frame, riding a bike without stabilizers, acquiring some knife skills in the kitchen or learning to drive a car. As long as whatever you're teaching is age-appropriate, however, this shouldn't deter you. Take sensible precautions, warn your child of any possible danger, reassure them that you'll be there for them if things don't quite go to plan, and encourage them to have a go.

When you're teaching a practical skill, it's much more fun for your child if they can be as 'hands on' as possible, getting stuck in at the thick end of things. This is a far more valuable experience than just being told what to do or watching someone else. Start off with a short demonstration, then step back and let them try. Allow them to set the pace to a certain extent so they feel properly involved, if not completely in control just yet. Ask for their ideas on how the process could be improved and let them try the most appropriate; it's through trial and error that they'll learn and remember what works and what doesn't.

You might decide there are some skills – like driving a car when the time comes, for instance – that are best left to the experts to teach your child, and this will depend on your own aptitude as well as your patience levels and the time and money you have available. If your child's keen to learn to drive, though, and is at an appropriate age, let them know you're actively looking for lessons. (Before you confirm this, though, consider whether or not you'll be happy either to provide them with a car of their own or let them use the family vehicle – and don't forget there'll be extra insurance and running costs to pay for, so they may need to make a contribution.)

If you decide to teach your child yourself, try to approach it positively so you're not barking at them all the time. 'I said right, not left!' or 'I've told you six times to press the clutch!' or 'Watch out!!!' aren't helpful, could cause an accident and won't make relations between the two of you any easier!

I got an unwelcome insight into my teaching skills when I saw Matthew bossing his Action Man around, saying 'No, don't do it like that, do it like this. Here, let me do it for you.' It was like listening to myself and brought me up short! I don't think I'd want to be taught anything in that way. At least it's made me more aware I need to let him try things for himself. I do struggle to resist the urge to wade in, but it's worth it to see Matt's sense of achievement afterwards.

Luca, dad to Matthew, six

Insight

Be prepared for the possibility that your child will be less cooperative when you're teaching them than they might be at school or elsewhere! They may well be more receptive to other adults as they won't feel as inclined to challenge their ideas. Try not to take this personally, and don't let it put you off introducing them to new skills.

How to build body confidence in your child

YOUNG CHILDREN AND TWEENIES

The issue of body confidence seems to occur frighteningly early in children's lives now. A recent report put the average age of the onset of puberty in girls at just nine years old, and one television documentary found that an awareness of body image can begin in girls from around six years old. There was also an inherent belief among the children studied in the documentary that skinny is best but average-sized or larger figures are unacceptable and even undesirable. It may be too late to undo the damage that's been exacerbated by media images of airbrushed models, the introduction of size zero clothing and the popularity of pre-teen magazines offering advice on how to be beautiful, but it's not too late for you to engender a different attitude within your home. Body consciousness isn't peculiar to girls either; boys can be equally self-critical, especially if they fail to develop at the same rate as their peers.

Because body consciousness begins so young in some children, it's worth trying to head off any avoidable issues. Childhood obesity, for instance, is on the rise and this can be blamed on the fact that children are relatively inactive compared with previous generations. This is partly because so many of the things kids like to do are screen-based and don't involve any physical exertion, and partly down to the fact that parents and guardians have become more wary than ever before of letting their children play unsupervised out of doors.

The best way to counteract or avoid the problem of being overweight (and not all children with a weight problem are clinically obese, just as not all children develop weight problems in any case) is to offer a good, well-balanced diet that includes fibrous fruit and vegetables; to limit sugary, fatty and salty snacks and drinks; and to encourage more physical activity. If children grow up with this lifestyle as the norm, they're more likely to keep up the good work instinctively later on. (And it won't do us adults any harm to adopt a healthier lifestyle either.) The key – as in other matters – is to allow a degree of freedom of choice and not to forbid 'unhealthy' foods altogether. Here are some pointers:

▶ Don't keep too many crisps, biscuits and other sugary, fatty or salty snacks in the house. If you do want to offer them, keep a small supply somewhere and limit how often you given them. Maybe you could have a jar of biscuits stashed away somewhere that you can hand out from time to time. Banning them outright will only make him crave them more.

▶ Get your child involved in counting her 'five a day' fruit and vegetables portions. You could have a star chart for them to complete each day, and perhaps they could get extra stars for trying something new.

▶ Try not to use food as a reward. Sweets and cakes given in return for good behaviour will make them seem precious and desirable. Giving them out with no strings attached will avoid this association.

▶ Make a game of exercising. Chase your child up the stairs; invest in a mini 'trampette' (a small indoor trampoline) and challenge them to beat their own record of bounces per minute; have a family dancing competition (yes, that means you as well!); set up some outdoor games that you can all play together; go on family bike rides at the weekends. You don't have to join up to a health club or fork out for swimming sessions all the time, although it's important to ring the changes occasionally so they don't get bored. In summer, for instance, see if there's an open-air lido near you – well-kept ones are great in good weather and don't cost much to use.

▶ Swap to lower-fat foods, not only for your child but for all of you (but only after they've reached the age of two). Bear in mind, though, that some of these will have extra sugar in them to compensate, so it's always worth reading the labels.

▶ Encourage your older child to make their own smoothies. A good basis is banana with milk or yogurt (try the low-fat flavoured yogurts as well as natural), and they could add berries, kiwis, mango, peach or other soft fruit and perhaps a little ice cream. There should be no need to add sugar, although a small drizzle of honey might help if the fruit isn't particularly sweet.

▶ Keep slices of melon chilled in the fridge. They'll keep for several days in a lidded plastic box and are handy for snacking on.

▶ Have a bumper tub of sweets under your control. This means you can ration them more effectively than handing over a bag and asking your child not to eat them all at once (imagine the control required to stop!).

▶ Bear in mind that children who appear to be naturally skinny are still vulnerable to the effects of eating the wrong foods. Some will maintain their small frames, while others will be more prone to gaining weight later on. One long-term research study which began in 1994 at Imperial College, London, shows that people who eat a fatty diet can appear healthily slim on the outside but can have dangerous levels of fat deposits around their organs, and this is very bad news for longer term health, raising the risk of developing diabetes and heart disease.

▶ With younger children, be a bit flexible about mealtimes: if you leave your child without food until they're starving hungry, they are more likely to overeat than if you give them healthy snacks throughout the day or bring mealtimes forward a bit.

If you think your child is a bit weighty for their age or height, you can check their BMI (body mass index) using an online calculator. This indicates what percentage of fat their weight is made up of and gives an idea of the range of weights that they're expected to fall within. It's worth considering, though, that lots of kids develop 'puppy fat' which means they're out of proportion for a while, and this is particularly true for girls, who lay down extra fat stores from the onset of puberty, but don't always grow in height at the same rate to compensate. In this case, point out that your child will soon shoot up in height and the excess weight will then be more evenly spread. If their BMI comes out very high, though, consider a visit to your GP to get them back on track.

What's just as important as trying to stave off weight problems is to make positive comments about your child to give them a good self-image. Focus on all their best physical attributes and praise their character. If they start to compare themselves with celebs in magazines or on television, discuss with them how images can be altered by the media and point out how many 'real' people actually fall way outside these ideals. Reassure them that you're more 'normal' if you don't fit a media stereotype than if you do! Explain that their body will go through lots of changes on the way to adulthood, all of which are quite normal, and that different children will change at different times. It's quite common, for instance, for some kids to have growth spurts which mean they're way taller than others of the same age – and a tall child can feel just as awkward as someone who's relatively short for their age.

TEENS AND YOUNG ADULTS

If your child is suffering from common problems like acne, dandruff or oily skin that can affect teens and young adults – or anything else that could threaten their body confidence – try to find ways of boosting their self-esteem. You could either offer them some products that might help or show them ways of disguising any blemishes. They probably won't believe you if you say 'Don't be daft, that spot's hardly noticeable' and will be mortified if you make light of it with ill-judged humour, but it'll help if you acknowledge what a pain it must be and then find ways to lessen the impact. If they have a severe case of acne, take it seriously and offer to go to the doctor with them: there are medical preparations that can help.

As with your younger child, draw attention to their best features whenever the opportunity arises (but not as an immediate response to their anxieties over their appearance, as that would be obvious and patronizing). Let them know you appreciate the pleasing aspects of their personality and any special skills they've got so that they feel valuable in other ways than purely physical (although it's important to realize, too, that peer and media pressure will probably mean that their appearance is their main concern, for now at least).

Bear in mind that your child might not confide in you about anxieties they may have over their appearance and they may come out as general bad temper or sulkiness; on the other hand, you might assume they're lacking in confidence because they have bad skin when in fact something else is on their mind – so it's important to tread carefully if you're thinking of bringing the subject up. Perhaps you could talk about your own experiences at their age and see what response that gets. It might give you an idea of whether or not they have any body confidence issues of their own or whether there's something else going on.

In any case it'll pay to be sympathetic to your child's likely sensitivities, and you can do this, for example, by respecting their wishes when it comes to being photographed, holding back on negative comments about their clothes or other image choices and never drawing attention to any obvious physical flaws in front of other people. (It's very easy to comment to a friend 'He's feeling a bit sensitive about that big spot on his nose,' but it's quite unlikely to make them feel any better about it and pretty likely to make things worse!)

EARLY SEXUAL EXPERIENCES

Body confidence becomes even more important as your older child begins to experiment sexually (and, however much you might resist the idea, it may happen sooner than you think or know). You can help by allowing them some privacy but making sure they realize that they can talk to you about anything. Don't embarrass them by opening up conversation after conversation about sex or trying to act the 'cool parent' by sharing experiences of your own early encounters. You could say something like 'I know things are changing a lot for you right now and if you want to talk anything through I'll always listen and will try never to judge you, so feel free.' And it's fine to remind them: 'I was your age not all that long ago; not that much changes when it comes to becoming an adult, so if you want to share, I'm here,' or 'Sometimes things don't always go quite as you're expecting them to when you're trying a new experience, so no need to be embarrassed if there's something you'd like to ask about.' (They'll probably just cringe and walk away, but the message will still have found its way home.) Don't worry or take offence if your child doesn't open up to you about the sexual experiences they may be having; they might have enough confidants among their own friends or might just be confident enough in themselves and in what you've already told them not to need any more advice.

You don't have to go as far as allowing girlfriends or boyfriends to sleep with your child under your roof if you're uncomfortable with this, but it might be a good idea to encourage them into your home and give them a bit of privacy so they don't feel they have to go to unsuitable places for a bit of intimacy.

Talking about eating disorders

Your child will probably be aware of eating disorders and these may have been discussed at school. It's a conversation that's worth having at home too, whether or not you suspect your child might have issues of their own. For a start, some children hear only parts of a message delivered in the context of a busy classroom. Maybe during a lesson on healthy eating, for instance, your child has latched on to the fact that 'fat is bad' and 'sugary sweets should be avoided'. You may notice your child's appetite for chocolate, crisps and chips seem to diminish – no bad thing, of course – but also that they start to examine every meal for signs of unhealthy ingredients. On the other hand, they might have latched on to a positive fact, such as 'eating five a day keeps you healthy', but if they start to become obsessive about how many pieces of fruit and vegetables they've had each day – which is quite different from taking an interest and doing their best – then they have misinterpreted the message and need some reassurance and clarification from you.

Peer pressure comes into play here, too, especially among girls, who may compete with each other by 'dieting'. Your daughter may be vulnerable to others telling her, for instance, that they've only had a handful of grapes or a low-cal cereal bar for breakfast, leaving her feeling that she's got to follow suit if she's going to remain slim or lose weight. Tell her that as long as her mates remain healthy-looking and are not visibly thin, it's unlikely they're existing on what they say they're eating, and that it's just a bit of showing off to impress their friends. Explain that as long as she eats three good, healthy meals and some sensible snacks plus a treat or two each day and stays active she won't put on excessive weight and will be healthier than a very thin girl, who may not be getting enough nutrients to grow and develop properly. Tell her, too, that girls who lose too much weight and starve themselves often become hairy in places where they don't want hair; bald in places where the should be growing it and tend to stop or never start having periods – so if she thinks she might want to have children of her own one day, it's important to let all that healthy development take place as and when her body is ready.

Boys too can be influenced by show-offs in their group; some boys start 'pumping iron' at an inappropriate age and do everything in their power to achieve the all-important 'six pack'. They thrive on power drinks and may even have found a way of getting hold of steroid drugs. Point out to your son that this is in no way normal development and that his mates are leaving themselves vulnerable to poor health and flab later on when they stop exercising quite so much.

Gavin had always been a couch potato, so when he asked to join a gym with his mates I was really pleased. It started off with a few running sessions but it wasn't long before he was into weights as well. We thought at first it was a bit of a macho thing, trying to build some muscles to impress his mates and the girls at school. Then he started getting up really early at weekends and spending far too much time at the gym, whether or not his friends were there. Within six months he was beginning to look a bit too muscle-bound so we went to the gym with him and got one of the personal trainers to devise a programme for him. There are some rest days built in and he's sticking with it, thank goodness. I've heard that exercise and weight training can become obsessive, but I think because a trainer has told him the way to go, he's happy with that.

Maria, mum to Gavin, 16

Insight

Instead of worrying yourself silly about your child's eating habits and trying to force meals on them, which will probably have a negative outcome, do something positive to help them feel better about themselves. If they want to become fit, encourage them to join a sports team out of school (as well as in); swim or cycle regularly; perhaps take up a martial art or join a gym and maintain a good diet. Explain that they'll need good nutrition in order to lose any fat and build muscle, and that starving themselves will only result in a loss of muscle as well as important body tissue.

COULD YOUR CHILD HAVE AN EATING DISORDER?

For some children, eating – or not eating – is a symptom of a deeper-seated problem. If a child doesn't feel empowered or listened to, for instance, or if they're troubled over things they feel are out of their control, they might decide – whether consciously or not – that food intake is one area of their life they can control. Signs to watch out for include:

▶ a noticeably smaller appetite than usual, continuing beyond several days and with no signs of illness
▶ excessive interest in weight
▶ faddiness over foods which were previously enjoyed
▶ hiding food to avoid eating it
▶ saying they're not hungry, even when they haven't eaten for hours
▶ not wanting to eat out
▶ losing weight
▶ over-exercising
▶ obsessing about unhealthy foods.

If you're concerned that your child's eating habits are changing and you think there may be an underlying problem, don't hesitate to take them to the doctor; early intervention often has better results than if an eating disorder is allowed to continue unchecked.

LEADING BY EXAMPLE

Much as your child – especially teenage or older – is unlikely to admit you're any kind of a role model when it comes to how you or your partner present yourselves, nevertheless they're probably influenced to some extent by your attitude towards your appearance, even if only subliminally! It's best if you can avoid being overly critical of yourself in front of them. Try to dress to your advantage (and age) and to maintain good posture: the way you carry yourself can have a big impact on how you look as well as how confident you appear to other people.

Set a good example by trying to exercise when you can. It doesn't have to mean thrashing up and down a pool or pumping iron at the gym; it could mean something as simple as walking to the local shops instead of driving.

Sit down with your family at mealtimes and eat a healthy meal. Don't try to exist on the heavily marketed 'slimming shakes' and cereal bars that promise fast weight loss. Just as your child needs to learn to keep their weight steady by eating the right things in the right proportions at the right time, you need to set it out as an easy-to-follow way of life. Don't keep hopping on and off the scales every morning bemoaning your weight gain or lack of loss – do it in private; avoid going on and on about how terrible you look in your jeans; try hard not to whinge about going to an exercise class if that's what you've committed to; and try to look and feel like you're happy in your own skin. They say that you can think yourself into a positive self-image by giving yourself regular affirmations each day, so if all else fails, try that!

10 THINGS TO REMEMBER

1 Play with your baby often; don't underestimate the capacity for learning in infancy.

2 Give your toddler regular, realistic challenges so that they feel they're accomplishing something a bit clever.

3 Identify your child's strengths and play to them by giving them opportunities to shine in what they're best at.

4 Talk to your child often and invite their opinions. It'll give them a sense of importance and value within the family.

5 Find age-appropriate responsibilities for your older child and help them get into the routine of doing them regularly.

6 Lead by example when it comes to showing your child how to appreciate other people's differences.

7 Review regularly how much freedom your child is allowed and adjust it whenever appropriate.

8 Take a deep breath as your tweenie enters puberty. (It may help to think back to your own behaviour when you were at their stage!)

9 Keep the lines of communication open between you and your teenager, even if you have to make all the running in conversations.

10 Be aware of the importance of building body confidence in your child; it's most likely to be very important to them.

5

Outside influences

In this chapter you will learn:
- *the importance of friendships*
- *equipping your child to combat bullying*
- *teaching personal safety*
- *how extra-curricular activities can boost confidence*
- *how spending time away can help your child blossom.*

Confidence in the wider world

However much you work on building up your child's self-esteem, the outside influences in their life will play an equally important part. For your child, it's important that they find a niche among their friends, both in and out of school and in any clubs they join. They may thrive as the leader of the pack or prefer to be a less prominent member of their band of mates, but as long as they find a position within the group that they're comfortable with, that's all that matters. Of course they'll want to be liked and appreciated by people other than immediate and extended family; in fact, they'll probably put more store by the approval of outsiders, and they're also likely to be more influenced by their opinions than they are by your unconditional love. This, in turn, can give rise to peer pressure that can be hard to resist, so you'll need to coach them in how to say no.

Other adults will influence your child too, from grandparents and neighbours to teachers, childminders, sports coaches and anyone else regularly involved in their life. Some will make positive contributions to their confidence; others might leave it a bit dented – and it'll be up to you to redress the balance. How much your child is influenced will, in part, depend on their own character: an outgoing, confident child is more likely to respond well to a vociferous, no-nonsense style of teaching, for example, than a shy child would be, and it will help if you bear this in mind when you're choosing after-school activities for them.

Their home life makes a difference as well. If yours is a home where, for instance, everyone has an equal right to their opinion and no one is afraid to voice it, they'll probably take criticisms and insensitive comments on the chin, but if they are used to a more reflective environment, they might take things other people say to heart more. It's probably better to teach them that there are many different sorts of personalities in the world and that they'll find ways of handling them all as they mature, than to try to protect them from characters who might rub them up the wrong way. It'll help them to grow in confidence and hone their social skills if they get used to viewing the world as a wonderfully diverse melting pot rather than seeing things outside of their own experience as being a bit scary. Having said that, try to make sure you spend more time with those people who empower them than with those who don't. Just as psychologists believe that for every criticism you level at your child you should give them five nuggets of praise, it also makes sense that if they have their confidence knocked, they'll benefit from lots of ego-boosting contact to make up for it.

Insight
One way of developing your child's engagement with the wider world is to take up a shared interest: maybe you could both join a martial arts or sketching class; perhaps you could join a gym or learn an instrument together; or you could have your own film or book club and make a regular date to go and see a movie together or read and discuss the same book.

BUILDING OUTSIDE RELATIONSHIPS

Your child will need your help learning the skills they need to build outside relationships. To some extent they'll learn from early on by watching how you interact with people outside of the home, so be aware of how you handle your friendships and how you deal with other people you come into contact with in daily life: schoolteachers, shop staff, other motorists, cold callers to your home, and so on.

An important skill to teach is the difference between being assertive or aggressive. One will help them to get their way skilfully; the other will rub everyone up the wrong way and even get them into trouble.

Assertiveness comes from self-assurance; aggression, on the other hand, can be defined as unprovoked offensiveness. Use role-play to show your child how to put their ideas across without being pushy, and how to get others to listen to them. For instance, ask them how they feel if you say 'Don't do it that way, do it this way, my way's best.' Then ask if it feels better when you say 'What if we try this? It might work better.' Get them to come up with some examples of their own. Young children can be very vocal and demanding, so you'll get lots of opportunities to suggest they think of a gentler way of asking for things. Next time he calls out 'I need a drink!', for instance, why not suggest they say 'Could you please bring me a drink?' instead.

> *Maddie got into a really bad habit of just shouting out whatever she needed, knowing that I'd come running. It was my fault for being so indulgent, but once she reached an age where she could sort herself out easily enough it started to wear thin. Now she's full of 'pleases' and 'thank yous' and it makes me feel proud when I hear her being so polite in other people's houses. They don't have to know I had to bribe her to get her into the habit!*
>
> Melanie, mum to Maddie, four

TAKING TURNS AND SHARING

Another vital skill to teach is turn-taking. Your child might be used to getting their own way most of the time at home, especially if they don't have siblings, but once they take up a place in a childcare setting or start school, they're going to have to learn pretty quickly how to wait their turn. Best if you coach them in this one before they make themselves unpopular outside of the home! Fun ways to show them are by playing board games and not letting your child 'just have one more go' when it's no longer their turn; taking it in turns to choose tracks on a CD; making sure everyone has equal amounts of time on the games console or trampoline when they have their friends round; setting an example by queuing patiently yourself in supermarkets (a real test of character, that one!); training your child to offer boxes of chocolates round to visitors first; and encouraging them to serve everyone else's potatoes at lunch before taking some for themselves.

TEACHING THEM TO SAY NO

In all your child's growing years, peer pressure will probably be one of the most difficult things to handle – for both of you. For them, it's important they feel part of the crowd and fit in; it's a rare child who wants to plough their own furrow early in life, and most want to be part of a wider group identity. For you, it'll be hard to stick to your principles on certain things once the pressure's on. In fact, it might be worth trying to stay a bit relaxed about issues that aren't vitally important. If you believe that children shouldn't be exposed to computer games that aren't aimed at their age group, then of course you should stick to your guns, but if you lay down the law about something a bit less serious, like whether or not you allow them to swap property with their friends, you'll probably find yourself at the centre of many an emotional battle and wonder whether it's really worth it. There's the added advantage, too, that if your child knows you're usually reasonable and flexible with your rules, they're more likely to respect you when you do put your foot down.

There will be times, though, when both you and your child would prefer them to say no to peer pressure. This can be tough, but it'll help if they understand that every person has the right to make their own individual choices about things and that it's perfectly OK to say no to anything they're uncomfortable with. They may be quizzed by their mates as to why, but your child doesn't have to justify their decision if they don't want to. Give them examples of when you have said 'no' to something; ask them what their attitude would be if one of their friends didn't want to go along with the crowd; get them to think of things they could offer the group as an alternative. So instead of just saying 'no', they could say '*OR* we could…'.

Your child will probably find it easiest to resist peer pressure at primary school age when you're still likely to be their biggest influence, but it usually grows increasingly problematic as children begin to grow away from their parents and see their peers as their main reference point. If you can help build a feeling of confidence in their own powers of decision making and let them know when you're impressed by their good decisions you'll help them maintain their individuality and they'll feel happier to stick their neck out when they're not comfortable with a situation.

In the end, peer pressure and your child's response to it is all part of growing up. It can be a nail-biting time, especially in teenage years, but rest assured that the majority of children go through a period of testing the boundaries, and most do eventually choose or return to family values.

I went mad at first when Rob said he wanted to get his ear pierced; it's not something we do in our family, and anyway he was only 11. I did let him get it done in the summer holidays because I sounded like the worst dad in the world saying no, but I was really unhappy about it. He kept the earring in for a few months, but then he changed friends at school and none of his new crowd had a piercing, so he let the hole close over. Just goes to show, what is vitally important to a kid one day can be totally uncool the next, depending on whose opinion matters. It's a bit gutting as a parent when you realize your views are regarded as embarrassing, but in my case it was very satisfying when he ditched the earring.

Rich, dad to Robert, 13

Insight

Resisting peer pressure is easier for all of us if we have support, and if your child has a good friend who's like-minded, the pair of them will find it easier to stand up for themselves than to go against the rest of the group individually. See if you can subtly encourage friendships with children who seem to share your family values. With the agreement of the friend's parents, talk to both children about how they might present a united front when they're uncomfortable with pressure from other friends.

Friendships and self-esteem

Friendships formed in childhood – although sometimes transient – can have a far-reaching effect in that they give us a kind of stamp of approval as valuable human beings. After all, if someone wants to be our friend, then we must be all right, and encouraging friendships among your child and their peers will help build their self-esteem as well as giving them an appreciation of different personality types. Being able to keep a friend takes empathy, sharing and democracy, which are all great skills for life too, so if your child can become good at making friends from early childhood they'll be well equipped for building healthy relationships in the future.

Good friendships give children the unbiased approval of their peers, which is quite different from the approval that comes from our unconditional love, so they're incredibly important to your child's self-esteem, especially as they begin to understand the difference between the two. It's been proven, too, that friendships are really crucial to self-esteem. Several US studies, for instance, have found an association between children's popularity and the quality of their friendships with their likelihood of developing depression later on.

AGES AND STAGES

For pre-schoolers, friends bring a sense of security to unfamiliar settings, such as nursery or playgroup, and they help your child understand that they're an individual person in their own right rather then being an extension of you. It'll be a few more years before they're really able to appreciate or understand the importance of their friendships, but this doesn't mean that they're not already contributing to your child's self-esteem and general happiness.

Once your child reaches junior-school age they'll have more of an idea of how their handling of friendships can affect their ups and downs. By this stage, although they'll appreciate the rubber-stamp effect their friendships can have on their confidence when they're going well, they'll be especially vulnerable to other people's opinions of them. If your child is in an unhappy situation, this will probably impact on their school performance, so it's really important to keep in touch with them about how their friendships are going.

If your child has the constancy of good friendships during their school years as well as later on at university and afterwards, they'll be able to cope much better with whatever disappointments or failures they may experience, and they'll have the pleasure of other people outside the family being there to celebrate their successes.

Friendships aren't all about what your child can get out of them, though: they also give your child lots of opportunities for being a supportive mate themselves, for helping to sort out disagreements within their friendship group and for appreciating other people's differences. Knowing they are a good mate will boost their confidence and give your child another sort of happiness and reward.

HOW TO HELP YOUR CHILD MAKE FRIENDS

The first thing we have to give our children in order for them to feel confident to approach other people is a sense of self worth, and your child will pick this up from babyhood onwards through their early experiences, home environment, family friends, relatives and teachers. It's only when they feel secure in themselves that they'll begin to appreciate the worth of others. But although young children tend to be uninhibited and non-judgemental in their earliest days, they usually need a bit of coaching in how to make friends and relate to their peers. If they don't get support and are left to make contact with other kids themselves, chances are they'll feel a bit intimidated and may even be full of self-doubt.

Put yourself in your child's shoes by imagining that you've been dropped off at a party where you don't know anyone. Maybe you thrive on this sort of social situation – and if you do, it's probably because you've been given the skills in childhood to break the ice and talk to new people. It's more likely, though, that you'll feel a bit out of your depth and be on the look-out for at least one person you recognize who might be able to make some introductions.

Try not to get panicky if your child chooses a friend or circle of mates you wouldn't have chosen for them yourself. As long as there's no dangerous behaviour going on and your child isn't being led down a path they're unhappy with, it's important that you allow them to choose their own friends. Once they're old enough to realize that you might be bothered, they could decide to get friendly with the 'wrong' bunch just to annoy you and assert their own independence. Don't worry, well-balanced children will often fall in with a less-than-desirable crowd for a while, but then get bored with the limitations of the friendships and come back round to your way of thinking (or at least something vaguely close to it!).

> *It was fantastic watching Emma growing in confidence as she made her first proper friendships. She'd played with a small group of children in Reception, but didn't really seem to care much about other kids until she was in Year 2. Now she's in Year 5 she still has the same best friend and group of mates, and they're usually quite supportive of each other. Of course, we do have the odd outbreaks of bitchiness, which seems to affect groups of girls more than boys, but I guess it's all part of normal development. At least when you fall out with one friend in a group you can still hang out with someone else.*
>
> Rachael, mum to Emma, ten

WHEN FRIENDSHIPS GO WRONG

It can't be all smooth sailing for your child, no matter how friendly and outgoing they are. Sooner or later (probably sooner) there'll be some upset or other that may seem devastating to them but trivial to you. No matter what your child's age, the best way you can help them is to encourage your child to talk about what's gone wrong and to really listen. You can make sure you're listening effectively by the reflecting technique – which, as described earlier in the book, means repeating back to them what they've just told you (although obviously not in exactly the same words). This will show them that you've understood properly. The next step is to help them think through why things went wrong and come up with suggestions for how they might be able to be put right. You can give them ideas for making up without admitting responsibility if they feel they haven't done anything wrong; if they know they're at fault, though, it's important they do apologize to their friend, and it's good practice for later relationships if they can do it face to face rather than by text, email or phone. It doesn't have to be a great big deal, and you can demonstrate how quick and easy it can be by making a point of apologizing yourself whenever you know you're in the wrong.

Sometimes friendships can be broken irretrievably, and even if your child hasn't come to this conclusion themselves, they might just have to accept it. Encourage them to make or strengthen other friendships, and make it easy for them to invite other mates into your home so it's not all down to how they act at school.

> *I don't think I've ever known such a succession of best mates as Jordan had during his early days in high school. I'd just get used to one lad when another new one would be brought home. It was probably to do with Jordan's changing tastes and the fact he joined a lot of quite diverse extra-curricular groups in school. We just welcomed whoever came through the door (and had a little worry to ourselves if it was a lad with lots of piercings or a big interest in Goth culture!). We didn't really need to get anxious though – Jordan ultimately felt most comfortable with people like him, and now his longer-standing friends feel more like an extension of our family – especially as they seem to sleep and eat here more than they do at home! One friend is even coming on our family summer holiday with us, which is great as Jordan, being an only child, could have been very bored or, worse still, have refused to come at all.*

Sally, mum to Jordan, 16

Resisting bullies

By law, all state schools in the UK have to have anti-bullying policies in place, but some cases will inevitably slip through the net or occur outside the school premises. In any case, there are all kinds of ways in which kids can be bullied, including online and by text as well as physically and verbally. As with making your child safe and aware of dangers on the internet, you have a responsibility to make them aware of what bullying means and how to respond if it happens to them. You need to make them aware, too, of the sorts of behaviour that could get them labelled a bully, and point out to them that what some people would consider teasing or playfulness, others would not.

At heart, bullies are cowards and it will empower your child if you bring them up believing this. Tell them that the person who stands up to a bully – whether directly or by reporting their behaviour – is the most likely to escape further incidents, while people who are easily intimidated will be picked on again and again. It's a sad fact, too, that bullies – because they are cowardly underneath the bravado – almost always target people they see as weaker than themselves, and will often pick on children with noticeable differences or specific areas of vulnerability.

If your child is bullied, whether in school or on the journey to or from school, the first step your child – or you – must take is to let a member of staff know. It might be helpful if you ask around other parents to see if they've heard of or experienced anything similar themselves: if you can get them to write in or sign a petition about any bullying they have witnessed it may make it easier for the head teacher to take steps to deal with the bully (or bullies). It's much harder to exclude pupils than it used to be, and suspensions are only for very limited times, but some schools do have exclusion zones where bullies can be segregated and educated away from the main school. Having said that, it's a fairly extreme measure, and it's better all round if the issue can be sorted promptly without resorting to 'school prison'!

It's worth telling your child that they don't have to choose to tell you or a teacher though: any trusted adult will do if they're happier with that, just as long as they tell someone. It's also a good idea to make them aware of online anti-bullying support websites and helplines; your child can also ask for help from them if they need to, and they don't have to give their real name.

It was mortifying to find out that Rebecca had been bullied for a whole term before I noticed anything was wrong. I was so preoccupied with my younger two moving up to middle school, and in any case I was expecting some mood swings and tantrums so I didn't even think to look into it any further. Then one of her friends' mums came over one weekend and told me that her daughter had told her Rebecca was scared stiff of a particular group of girls at the school. I went for a meeting with the head teacher who said she'd take action straight away. The girls concerned had apparently been accused of bullying before and were kept in the school's exclusion zone for a few weeks. After that they left Rebecca alone and, although she remained nervous for a couple of months, I noticed an improvement in her mood almost immediately. I just feel sad that I didn't notice my own daughter was in trouble and she didn't feel able to tell me.

Sofia, mum to Rebecca, 12, and twins Tom and Heather, eight

Some signs that your child might be being bullied include:

- ▶ coming home with minor injuries or ripped clothes
- ▶ repeatedly 'losing' dinner money or other valuables
- ▶ falling out with friends
- ▶ being bad-tempered without explanation
- ▶ becoming moodier than usual
- ▶ not wanting to eat
- ▶ regularly complaining of sickness on school days
- ▶ not wanting to go out
- ▶ suffering from interrupted sleep patterns
- ▶ falling behind with school work or doing less well than usual.

ONLINE OR TEXT BULLYING

If you suspect your child is being bullied by text or online, you will only be able to confirm this if they're confident about telling you, or if you practise a little deceit by monitoring their social networking conversations and phone messages. Be very careful before you go snooping, though, as you risk destroying your child's trust in you, and they may find ways of covering their tracks instead of opening up. It would be better, before you first let them have a social networking account and mobile phone, to say they can only have these privileges on condition they let you have access to their exchanges. They might resist, but if it's the only way they're going to get their way they'll probably agree. This can only be a fairly short-term measure, though, as once they become a teenager they'll not only start to demand their privacy, they'll be entitled to it. Hopefully by then they will be more streetwise about bullying, and the school will also have had some input in educating your child and their peers about personal safety.

Insight

The secrecy of bullying online or by text is another horrifying reality, but you'll have to accept that you can't monitor your child's every movement or communication, and that they may choose not to confide in you about being bullied because it could injure their pride. By the time your child becomes a teenager you'll both have to take each other on trust to some extent. That's the time to become extra vigilant for signs that something's not right (see the 'Some signs that your child might be being bullied' boxed text opposite).

Personal safety

Personal safety is now taught in primary and high schools, under the banner of PSHE (Personal, Social and Health Education, also known as PACE, PSE or PSHCE in some schools). The curriculum for PSHE follows guidelines laid down by the government and covers a wide range of subjects including nutrition and physical activity; drugs and alcohol; emotional health and wellbeing; sex and relationships; personal finance; safety; careers education and work-related learning.

However much the school educates your child in PSHE though, it doesn't cancel out your own parental responsibility to teach them about all these aspects of life yourself, especially their own personal safety. Your own experience is invaluable in making it all seem more relevant, and it's never too soon to start. Pre-schoolers tend to respond well to role-play, so use a range of teddies and dolls to play out situations involving 'stranger danger' and the boundaries of acceptable (or non-acceptable) behaviour. Stress to your child the importance of reporting to a trusted adult any inappropriate behaviour towards them by another adult or older child.

With older children you can build on what they're covering in school by discussing the subjects further, and by putting them into context with more examples from your own experience. If your child is reluctant to talk and won't tell you where they got up to at school with PSHE, you can always contact their teacher to ask for a schedule of what's being covered when. In any case, you're very likely to get a notification and be asked to sign a permission slip when sex education is about to be taught in school, and you may be invited to see for yourself what the coverage will involve. You will also have the opportunity to opt your child out if they are under 15. (See Chapter 4 for advice on how to talk to your child about sex.)

Remember: empowered children are confident children, and confident children are happy children. It might help to repeat this like a mantra whenever you're about to tackle an awkward or uncomfortable conversation with your child. You might find it helpful to get some resource material together first, either from the library or online.

Insight

Given the unpalatable fact that the sorts of dangers children fall prey to, such as physical and sexual abuse, are more often than not perpetrated by someone known to them, it's vital to spot the signs early. With younger children, role-play is useful again. You don't have to be explicit, but you may get a feel for whether or not there is any cause for concern if you say, for example: 'Look at how Teddy is getting really close to your dolly. Do you think she likes that or not?' or 'What do you think Teddy is going to do next?' If your child says something innocent sounding, like 'Cuddle her', ask her 'And do you think your dolly will want him to? Will she like that? Who do you think she'll tell about it afterwards?' If you do have any reason to suspect abuse – and the very fact that you are testing the water with your child means your gut instinct tells you something is wrong – call the NSPCC child protection helpline on 0808 800 5000 or email help@nspcc.org.uk to discuss your concerns. They will advise you on what to do next.

IMPORTANT STEPS YOU CAN TAKE TO PROTECT YOUR CHILD

There are things you can do to further protect your child:

▶ Make sure you have set parental controls on all your PCs and laptops so that the range of material they can view online is restricted.

- ▶ Keep the PC downstairs in a family room or in the kitchen or hallway rather than in your child's room so that you can – even surreptitiously – keep an eye on what they're looking at.
- ▶ Teach them never to expose their real identity or any personal details to any stranger online, nor to trust anyone they don't know – even if they claim to be a friend of a friend. They must verify all information, with your help if necessary, before communicating with any newcomers.
- ▶ Explain to your child about 'grooming' – i.e. how some individuals will pose as children or young adults themselves, including posting a fake photo online, in order to win the trust of children. They will then try to set up a meeting in secret, and this can lead to abuse, abduction or worse. It may seem a harsh message to deliver, but it's vital you do so. (Remember how you thought you knew everything when you were a kid? And how it took until you were an adult to realize that you didn't?)

How clubs boost confidence

Signing your child up to some after-school clubs can give them a fantastic boost, especially if you find something they excel in that isn't offered at school. Supposing, for instance, you discover that they've got a real talent for golf or archery, photography or judo? It'll give them a chance to achieve out of school, as well as providing another source of new friendships. It doesn't have to be anything competitive, as long as they have opportunities to progress.

Clubs can be particularly confidence-boosting for children who don't shine academically or aren't likely to make it to Team Captain in sports. Finding something your child's got a natural aptitude for will increase their sense of individuality, develop in them a sense of pride and give them a skill other children in their circle don't have, thus making your child an 'expert' in their own field.

Attending clubs regularly has other advantages too: it can mean making a commitment; being punctual; performing to a standard; interacting with other peers and adults; learning to respect the authority of others; working as a team; keeping a uniform smart; abiding by another set of rules and paying attention to their own fitness. All this adds up to a big injection of self-esteem – and gives them something new to talk to other people about as well.

Callum has always coasted along in the middle-ability groups at school and never really been sporty. When he said he'd like to learn the trumpet, to be honest I thought it would be a one-term wonder, but he's really taken to it and has genuine flair. His teacher has suggested he try out for a local band, which would mean public performances and a bit of touring, and just the suggestion has done his self-confidence a power of good. He loves practising (not sure whether the neighbours relish it much!) and has taken Grade 1 already – that's in just one year. I think it's a good instrument for him to have chosen because it's quite 'macho'. He's performed at a couple of school assemblies and you can just see that his friends are full of admiration. I'd really encourage other parents to try their children out with different hobbies as you never know when you're going to strike gold.

Lucy, mum to Callum, nine

How time apart builds confidence

Babies and pre-schoolers

The first time you separate from your child is always likely to cause a bit of stress all round, so it's a great idea to have them sleep over with friends or relatives from when they're young enough to cope so that it becomes the norm. If you have parents who live nearby, this is probably a good place to start as your child's grandparents' house will already be familiar to them. You could leave a few toys, games and DVDs there so that they always feel it's a home from home.

If you're not comfortable with anyone else caring for your child overnight, or if it's just not practical, start by arranging a 'child swap' where a friend looks after them for the afternoon with her own child and then you return the favour. Being with other trusted adults will open up the scope of your child's experience so that they don't always expect everything to be exactly the same as at home. It'll be good for them to have to muck in with other people's routines – and it's worth pointing out that, just as Granny's rules apply in her home but not necessarily yours, the same is true of other friends' homes as well. Introducing these small separations before they start childcare or school will prepare them for a longer time spent away from you, and they'll already have confidence that although you leave them, you always come back for them later on.

School-age children

It probably won't be long after your child starts school that the first sleepover invitation comes home. Don't think you have to agree if you don't know the family well; most parents understand that others will want to know a bit about them and how their household operates before entrusting a child to their care. See if you can arrange a get-together beforehand, even if it's just a coffee at their friend's house. You'll probably be able to gauge whether or not you're happy with the set-up within a fairly short time. If you don't feel comfortable with the arrangement, you can always make the excuse that your child has got cold feet at the last minute. This means explaining to your child why they can't go on the sleepover – perhaps you could say that you're the one who's not ready to leave them overnight just yet.

Whenever you do agree to that first night away from home, do so with confidence and try not to fuss over your child. They'll get on perfectly well once they're ensconced with their friend. You might want to check with them whether or not they'd prefer to take something from home – their own pillow perhaps, and their favourite cuddly toy – so that they have something familiar to cuddle up with at bedtime. Apart from that, a quick phone call just before your child goes to bed might be a good thing, unless you suspect that this is more likely to make them homesick. Otherwise, why not suggest to the other child's mum that she offers for them to call you if they'd like to. The key is to set the mood yourself by being relaxed and happy as you leave them. They'll feel happier to trust their friend's family if they can see that you do. Make sure you arrive promptly to collect them the next day. They'll either be more than ready to come home or reluctant to leave; either way you'll have done the right thing.

PREPARING FOR A SCHOOL TRIP

Day trips from school are one thing your child will quickly get used to – as long as you make sure the staff know if they're likely to be travel sick and that you take steps to prevent it as far as possible. Residential trips are something else and often take place in Year 6, in preparation for the greater responsibility and separation your child will experience when they start high school. The majority of children – even those who seem anxious and reluctant about staying away from home – thrive on these trips and come back full of new-found independence and the confidence that brings. Don't forget that the teachers will probably have run this trip many times before and will have good experience of what works and what doesn't – both practically and emotionally.

As with early separations, the key is to embrace the idea yourself. You're probably going to feel your child's absence more acutely than they feel yours once they've found their way around their new accommodation and get the idea of the new routine, so if you're anxious, try not to show it in front of them, and remember that time spent apart usually makes for a greater appreciation of each other when the separation is over.

If they're nervous about going away, it's best not to 'big up' the trip the whole time, but chat to them in a low-key way about the fun they're going to have and how it'll be a bit like a big sleepover, but with more of their friends than you could possibly accommodate at home! Reassure them with cuddles, and ask them if they've got any specific worries so that you can talk to their teachers and find ways to overcome potential problems. If there are issues you're aware of that might upset them – such as if your child sleepwalks or tends to wet the bed when they're away from home – let the teachers know in advance. They'll have coping strategies and will be able to reassure you – and you in turn can reassure your child. Don't say to them 'Of course you'll be all right. You're a big boy now!' Do allow them to regress a bit in the run-up if it makes them feel safer about going.

There will be meetings arranged by the school beforehand where you'll have all the information you need about contact arrangements; what to do if your child has a medical condition; what they should take with them and what they should definitely leave behind! Do take good notice of the rules: if the school says it prefers children not to bring hand-held computer games, leave them at home. Otherwise you risk your child's getting lost, stolen or broken, which will be the reason behind the rule in the first place.

Amber was looking forward to the school trip in the run-up, but about a week before she was due to go she suddenly got cold feet and said she didn't want to go without me. I think it was the thought of no contact for almost a week that was disturbing her, so I told her I would leave a note for every night, labelled with each day, for her to open before she went to sleep. The school had organized for parents to send a letter in to the school office

*before they left, which would be handed out to each child on the
first day, too, but the children weren't to know about that one in
advance, so it was an extra surprise for Amber. We talked about
the fact that the staff would have all the parents' contact details
and would, of course, ring us if anything was really wrong.
She was still a bit clingy when we left her on the coach, but the
staff sent daily updates to the school, which were displayed on
an LCD screen in the hall, so I went in each afternoon to see
what they had to say. I needn't have worried – when we went to
collect Amber on the Friday evening, she said she'd have been .
quite happy to stay an extra night!*

Danni, mum to Amber, 11

Insight

You should expect to greet a slightly more grown-up child when they return
from the trip, but there's no need to worry that they won't need you any
more. OK, so they might come home full of bravado and ready to test the
boundaries again, but that's all part of growing up, and they'll still need your
comfort and guidance for many years to come. In the meantime, you can
capitalize on all their new skills and feel proud that your child is developing
and maturing in readiness for the challenges of high school and beyond.

10 THINGS TO REMEMBER

1 Teach your child the difference between being aggressive and being assertive.

2 Instil the idea of turn-taking by playing board games and getting them to wait a bit before answering their demands.

3 Allow them to choose their own friends, even if you don't necessarily approve of them; it's important for their self-esteem.

4 Teach them how to say no when they're uncomfortable with a group suggestion.

5 Encourage one-to-one friendships by asking their close mates home regularly.

6 Take action promptly if you suspect your child – or any child – is being bullied.

7 Take steps to protect them online: set parental controls and keep the PC in a family room.

8 Use role-play to talk about difficult issues.

9 Give your child opportunities to shine outside of school by joining them up with some clubs that nurture other interests.

10 Set the mood for their school trip by being a grown-up about it yourself!

6

Rebuilding confidence after a crisis

In this chapter you will learn:
- *how to spot a downturn in confidence*
- *some reasons for a sudden crisis of confidence*
- *how to start rebuilding your child's confidence*
- *how to move on from the crisis*
- *how to spot depression in your child.*

When confidence is threatened

However well your child seems to be doing and however much confidence you can see they've gained, there may be times when they suffer periods of self-doubt, whether brought on by themselves or by others, deliberately or otherwise. Their confidence at any age, even as a school-leaver, may still be quite fragile and easily knocked. So if, for instance, their judgement is called into question or mocked – whether it's over a rock band, an idea for how to spend the weekend, their new outfit or a political issue – they may become a bit introspective and start to feel unsure of their ability to make 'good' choices. This is another time you can reassure them that they are an individual person in their own right, and that their choices reflect their very valid opinions and tastes, so are not to be mocked or disrespected. Don't go over the top enthusing about your child's new ripped-jeans look or out-there hair colour, though, or they'll sense your insincerity (desperation, even?) and will either switch off or panic.

Signs that your child could be suffering a crisis of confidence include:

▶ being generally low-spirited
▶ seeking lots of reassurance about trivial things
▶ mistrusting their own judgement (for instance, being unhappy with clothes they previously felt comfortable wearing)
▶ seeing less of their friends
▶ finding less to tell you about that's been fun for them
▶ performing less well in school
▶ wanting to drop out of some of their out-of-school clubs (although this is a fairly typical development for children as they reach high school age in any case!).

Ciara was getting on so well at school and always wanted friends back home; we were really pleased with how happy she seemed. But there was one half-term holiday when she discovered that some of her friends had had several get-togethers without her, and that really seemed to knock her confidence. The first sign was not wanting to go back to school after the holiday, which I could understand, but we got her over that. Then we got a call from her teacher saying she didn't seem to want to interact with her usual group of friends and the next thing was she turned down an invitation to one of her best mates' parties. We sat and talked together about what she thought was behind not being invited out during half term. Ciara thought she must have offended or upset someone in the group, although she hadn't actually checked this with any of them, but after a couple of phone calls to the mums I knew well, I soon found out that the others had thought we were away at half term. Someone got the wrong end of the stick and they hadn't meant to exclude Ciara at all. At first Ciara didn't believe it, but a couple of days later she was back into bringing some stragglers home with her again!

Mandy, mum to Ciara, eight

WHAT'S BEHIND THE LOSS OF CONFIDENCE?

Before you start to explore how to rebuild your child's confidence, it'll help if you can work out what might be behind the crisis – that's if your child isn't reluctant to discuss it or to admit there's anything wrong. Reasons could include:

▶ body confidence and hormonal activity affecting their mood
▶ a disagreement with friends

- ▶ being bullied
- ▶ moving into a new area
- ▶ poor results at school
- ▶ a change in your family situation (even if not particularly recent)
- ▶ bereavement (even if not particularly recent)
- ▶ changes to their physical appearance.

Insight

It might not seem obvious where the problem lies at first; your child might not want to talk about whatever has upset them, especially if it involves their friends or if they are being bullied. (You can find advice on bullying in Chapter 5.) You'll need to approach things gently, perhaps by saying you've noticed they are not quite themselves and you're sure that even telling you a bit about it will make them feel better. Or perhaps your child would feel easier discussing it with their dad, an older sibling or a trusted family friend or teacher?

WORKING THROUGH THE CAUSES

Body confidence and hormones

Body confidence issues and the rather haphazard influx of hormones into your child's system can all undermine their confidence as they start puberty, especially if other children (or thoughtless adults) make fun of them. Remember: children can become pre-pubescent from as early as age seven, so talk to them periodically about what to expect, and explain that even quite irrational feelings can be normal during this time of physical adjustment. You'll find more tips on building body confidence and dealing with hormonal upheaval in Chapter 4.

House and/or school move

Moving house can be very exciting for all the family, and will probably be especially so for your child if they have a better bedroom and more space generally than before. But if you've moved far enough away to affect their friendships or to mean a change of school, they are very likely to become unsettled at some point. You might think you've got away with it if they seem happy and settled soon after moving, but it might be only after the novelty has worn off that the full impact hits home. You can ease their upset by keeping contact up with their former pals. If you're close enough for weekend visits, pencil in a few on the calendar and keep these dates available in case they want to organize a sleepover; if the distance is too far for this, tell your child you'll happily organize for someone to come and stay with you during the half-term or longer school holidays. Let them phone their friends regularly until they are more 'in' with their new crowd. It probably won't be long before they're ready to move on from old friendships – and even if they want to stay in touch, your child will soon find a new group of mates who'll come to mean as much to them or more.

Divorce or separation

If you're going through or have been through a change in your family circumstances, such as divorce or separation, your child might well try to 'cope' by seeming to be fine for fear of upsetting you even more than you're already suffering. Children can be incredibly perceptive and sensitive to their parents' anxiety and are good at putting a brave face on things if they think it'll help. This might be especially true if your child secretly believes that they may be the cause of the break-up – another horribly common misconception among children whose parents are splitting up. Again, even if your child seems fine at first, they may begin to crumble further down the line, especially when they realize that the split is likely to be permanent, and even more so if you have the extra upset of a change of house and/or school. They may have worries and concerns about the parent who's now living alone; or it may be that, for whatever reason, that parent is no longer in their life or has limited access, which will feel something like bereavement.

Helping your child cope with divorce or separation

The NSPCC offers the following very valuable insights into how you can ease the pain of divorce or separation for your child.

▶ Resist the temptation to treat your child as your confidant.
▶ Don't talk unfavourably about your ex-partner in front of your child.
▶ Do try to keep communication open with your ex-partner if possible, and agree reasonable access.
▶ Try to stick to regular access days and times so your ex-partner can plan for your child's visits.
▶ Don't react immediately if your child announces that they want to live with their other parent, or says they don't want to keep up contact.

▶ Any contact is usually better than none, but when regular visits aren't possible, letters, photos, cards and phone calls help make your child feel cared about by the absent parent.

▶ You may find it helpful to contact a group of other lone parents, such as Gingerbread or your own community group.

If you have serious concerns about your child's adjustment to the situation, talk to your health visitor, GP or school about a referral to your local NHS Child and Family Guidance Centre. The NSPCC publishes a range of very useful downloadable leaflets around divorce and separation on its website: www.nspcc.org.uk

Bereavement

Sometimes the loss of a family member – even a distant one – might affect your child more deeply than you imagine. Death often holds a morbid fascination even for quite young children, and if it's among their first experiences of bereavement, it will very likely raise questions in your child's mind about mortality – maybe not their own (children can be pretty egocentric and it can take quite a lot of life experience before they realize that they're not invincible), but perhaps yours or your partner's. Have a chat about how death is part of the natural order of things and that sometimes even relatively young people can die, but that this is not the norm and usually people live into old age. Explain that as people age they generally begin to accept the idea of dying one day, and that it isn't always the horrible trauma that kids are liable to imagine. You might find a book on how to explain death to children useful: good titles include *Water Bugs and Dragonflies: Explaining Death to Young Children* by Doris Stickney; *Sad Isn't Bad: A Good-Grief Guidebook for Kids Dealing with Loss (Elf-Help Books for Kids)* by Michaelene Mundy; *Always and Forever* by Alan Durant, and *Badger's Parting Gifts* by Susan Varley.

When my mum died suddenly – literally overnight and without warning – I didn't realize what an impact it would have on Natasha, who was only four at the time. I tried to keep myself together when she was around and did most of my grieving during the night. To my relief she seemed fine (although part of me wanted her to acknowledge what a huge loss it was for me). We took her to the funeral and had some lovely child-friendly hymns to lift her spirits, and she seemed really happy on the day and afterwards. Then, a couple of weeks later, she became very subdued and anxious and wouldn't sleep. She kept coming in to our room in the middle of the night looking for cuddles. After some probing by her dad, it turned out that she was really worried I might suddenly die, too, and she was coming in to check I was still breathing. I'd thought I was doing the right thing telling her 'Grandma just fell asleep and didn't wake up' as that was the truth and sounded quite untraumatic, but what I hadn't bargained for was her assuming that the same thing could happen to anyone at any time. My bereavement counsellor gave me some really good exercises to do with Natasha and she gradually got over the idea that I was about to die every time I nodded off, but at the time she was really emotionally fragile and seemed to lose her confidence in all sorts of ways.

Hayley, mum to Natasha, seven

Insight

Rebuilding your child's confidence after a break-up or bereavement will depend upon you being strong and showing a positive attitude, which might be very hard for you to manage. This doesn't mean, though, that you should try to conceal your upset from your child, who needs to know that it's normal to grieve or to feel sad that things haven't worked out as you'd hoped. It might be helpful to get your child some professional support from a counsellor if they find it hard to open up to you, your partner or another trusted adult. It may be that they don't want to 'burden' you with their own feelings when they can see that you have a lot to deal with yourself. Ask your child's head teacher or your GP to put you in touch with someone if you can't persuade them that you can take on their upset too, or if you yourself feel unable to offer them the right kind of support.

Rebuilding confidence with your child

Helping your child to regain confidence may take some time and will need your commitment. Spending extra time with them will help, although it's important not to force the issue and become overbearing, nor to make them feel like a victim. They just need to know that they're loved and appreciated, and that they have a lot of worthwhile things to contribute. Here are some ways you can help your child.

ALLOW THEM TO REGRESS

Everyone who has taken a confidence knock can feel a bit childlike about the whole experience. (Just think about all the comedies you've watched where grown men, when humiliated, have cried 'I want my mum!') It's just the same for kids of all ages – and it's quite normal for upsets to result in the need to be babied a bit. The sorts of ways your child might show regression are:

In a young child:

- ▶ carrying around a long-discarded comforter
- ▶ bedwetting or asking for a nappy
- ▶ asking for a dummy
- ▶ wanting you to feed them
- ▶ resuming thumb-sucking.

In an older child:

- ▶ sticking more closely to you than previously
- ▶ wanting things done for them that they are perfectly capable of doing for themselves
- ▶ needing extra reassurance
- ▶ wanting lots more cuddles, especially at night time
- ▶ seeming reluctant to be around their friends
- ▶ watching television programmes – especially old, familiar ones – aimed at younger children.

TAKE TIME TO LISTEN

Listening to your child and making opportunities for them to open up to you is the most valuable gift you can give them, particularly when their confidence is threatened. Proper listening entails much more than simply hearing and understanding what your child has to say, and is an important skill for life. To be effective, it should involve the reflecting technique described earlier in the book, which means repeating back the key messages you've heard. In order to really listen:

- ▶ set aside some specific time to spend with your child
- ▶ avoid any distractions – so switch off the television, ignore the phone and turn off your mobiles
- ▶ ask open-ended questions, requiring more than just 'yes' or 'no' answers
- ▶ allow your child to talk for as long as they want without interruption
- ▶ take opportunities to 'reflect', and be specific: for example, say 'So overhearing unkind things about yourself has made you

feel really sad' or 'I can understand why being left out of games makes you feel unhappy'

▶ let your child know you are always willing to listen to them, and that if you're busy you'll find time for them as soon as you can

▶ in tricky conversations, allow for some disrespectful comments and – in older children – even colourful language, and try not to react; the important thing is to listen to the message behind the anger, which is often a cry for help

▶ give your child, lots of hugs and love, if they welcome this

▶ always remember that you're the grown-up and behave accordingly!

By listening to your child, you're showing them that you care enough to take time out for them, that what they think and feel is really important to you and that they are special enough for you to put them first. That in itself is confidence boosting.

MAKE YOUR CHILD FEEL IMPORTANT

You can build up your child's sense of self worth and importance by giving them a few new responsibilities for things at home. Tell them they have really impressed you with all the stuff they do so well already, so you'd really appreciate their help with a few extras. Don't push it if the idea doesn't appeal to them – just knowing you're impressed with them will give your child's confidence a boost. If they do rise to the challenge, there's no need to follow them around praising every little thing they do, but do make sure you show them some appreciation, especially at the end of any task.

I asked Sam if he'd like to help his dad wash the car at the weekends now he was getting such a big boy, and he really took his new role seriously. His dad got some cheapo T-shirts printed with 'Car washer 1' and 'Car washer 2' for them to wear, and gave Sam his own special brush for cleaning the wheels and a chamois leather for polishing the wing mirrors – and he was chuffed to bits. It's probably because the chore was a more 'manly' one that he felt all puffed up with pride – especially when his dad told him he wouldn't want to do it by himself any more now that Sam was doing such a professional job. In fact Sam's even said he wants to be a car washer when he grows up!

Lizzie, mum to Sam, six

Insight

With a younger child, setting aside time to play more frequently or just sit and share a DVD and a cuddle will make your child feel special and valued. It sounds simple and obvious, but actually it's so much easier just to leave children in front of the television while we catch up with chores that it may not come automatically. And you could make a point sometimes of cooking their favourite tea or treating them to something special with no other reason than that you love and appreciate them.

RAISE THEIR SELF-ESTEEM

If your older child has issues with body confidence or their image, how about taking them on a shopping spree to kit them out with some new gear? They may not want to be seen around town with their mum though, so maybe you could enlist the help of an admired family friend or relative? Or perhaps, if they're old enough to go shopping independently, a school friend (whose style doesn't make you want to lie down in a darkened room) wouldn't mind helping your child choose?

It's a good time in general to give your child opportunities to practise things they're already good at; after all, which one of us doesn't get a real buzz from excelling at stuff? So, depending on their age, whether it's reading aloud to you, riding their bike, playing sport or beating you on the games console – whatever it might be – encourage your child to do it more often. Maybe they could take a hobby to the next level to help them feel they're achieving more – but be careful not to push them too far or too hard or they could end up failing, and that will only make them feel deflated.

I joined Josh up to a couple of clubs around things I already knew he was good at: one was a chess club that happens after school, and another was a diving club at the local swimming baths. His dad taught him to play chess when he was little, and he's always had a good, analytical type of brain, which has made him quite insular, meaning he finds it less easy to make friends than more boisterous kids. He's thriving at the club and has some of the other boys round to play chess with him at weekends. He's getting involved in a tournament, too. The diving seemed a natural choice for a really strong swimmer, and although Josh was a bit nervous about it at first, he's found he really loves it – and the children there are all a bit more outgoing so it offers him a different kind of involvement.

He seems a lot happier and is always ready to talk about his clubs, whereas he was very quiet before.

Alexandra, mum to Josh, 11

FIRE UP THEIR PASSION

Even just talking with your child about things they're really passionate about will fire up their enthusiasm and make them feel knowledgeable. Ask your child to talk you through their latest computer game and how you get through the levels; if they're into a particular sport get them to tell you all about their favourite player; maybe they have a big passion for wildlife and can tell you all about where their different animals live and how they survive.

> **Insight**
> With a very young child who seems to be having a confidence crisis, you'll need to go back to basics to build them up again. So remind them of all the things they've mastered since they were a baby and tell them how proud you are of all their achievements. Ask for their help with simple tasks around the house, like finding everyone a spoon for pudding or handing you the pegs when you're hanging out the washing. Give them lots of kisses and cuddles and tell your child how much you love them.

Moving on after a broken friendship

Suddenly finding themselves without a particular mate or circle of friends because of an irreparable falling out can be equally devastating for a young child with only a very young friendship as it can to an older child with more established relationships. Plus, the younger child – although admittedly probably more fickle – has less experience of how to move on after break-ups and how to go about finding a new niche in the school playground or outside. So, whatever the age of your child, they will probably need, or at least appreciate, some help with getting past their upset and finding new things to look forward to. Here's how you can help at each stage.

YOUR YOUNGER CHILD

If your child is primary-school age (and friendships usually only take on real significance from this point onwards), they'll have the advantage that their school world is relatively small, so the chances are they'll know all the children in their year group as well as some from the year above or below. This means that, perhaps with help from you, their teacher and/or other mums you know, they shouldn't find it too difficult to break into a new little gang if they aren't part of the old one any more. Of course, their old crowd will still be very visible and present every day, which might be hard at first, but a few weeks of mixing with and getting to know a different set of children better will probably be all they need to feel comfortable again.

If it's just one friend they have fallen out with, it's likely that one or the other will change groups or that the old crowd will dissipate into smaller groups because the dynamic will have changed. If they have enjoyed friendships with more than one group of kids throughout their time in school so far, the problem will probably be less intense and you may be surprised by how easily they swap allegiance.

You can help by:

▶ suggesting they bring one or two friends from their new group home for tea
▶ asking them whether they think their old friendship/s might work better out of the school setting, in which case perhaps some of them could join an after-school activity together or they could ask them individually for sleepovers
▶ keeping in touch with your child's teacher to find out how any new friendships are progressing and old upsets resolved
▶ keeping your eyes open for sudden changes in your child's mood or behaviour that might suggest they're still not happy
▶ talking and listening to them, using the reflecting technique described earlier in the book
▶ helping your child to find ways of resolving conflicts themselves.

It was really upsetting for Chloe when her best friend suddenly went off with a child whose mum had become friends with hers. Chloe's friend and this other girl were spending more and more time with each outside of school because the mums were meeting up all the time, so it was pretty inevitable that they'd become close, but it left Chloe wondering what she'd done wrong. At her age, it was hard to explain the concept that convenience can sometimes be all that's needed for friendships to grow (like some of the antenatal and postnatal friendships new mums make, for instance), but on the other hand I didn't want her to bad-mouth her friend or for there to be any ill feeling.

Anyway, I needn't have worried; within a week Chloe had a new best friend of her own. As luck would have it, a new child joined the school and her teacher, seeing what had happened, asked Chloe to be the new girl's buddy for a while. They're inseparable now! I've also encouraged Chloe to ask a few other kids back for play sessions after school so that instead of having just one really good friend she has lots to turn to if things go a bit wrong.

Mags, mum to Chloe, five

> **Insight**
>
> Sometimes children who become estranged from each other within a group of friends will rekindle that friendship when they're no longer spending a lot of time together, even if it takes time. After all, whatever it was that attracted them to each other is likely to remain, and they might enjoy an easier friendship than before if they don't feel under pressure from one another to spend all their time together.

YOUR OLDER CHILD

It's different for a high school child when it comes to making up and breaking up friendships. Depending on where you live, your child might find themselves one of many hundreds of pupils – in some cases over 1,000. This can mean their friendship group is even more important to them because there are so many cliques formed at this stage that it can be hard to get in with other kids. Your child might, if their school operates a setting system, find that they have one group of pals in their form and another in their set, so this gives more opportunities for forming new relationships. Also, by pre-teen and teenage years, they'll probably place great importance on what their friends think of them, so a break-up might hit them hard. Worse still, they might feel embarrassed or ashamed and not want to tell you about it.

It's not unusual for this age group to have frequent periods of being uncommunicative or sulky, so you might have to look for other signs that something has gone wrong, such as noting how many texts your child is receiving compared with usual; monitoring any social networking pages they have (you should do this as a matter of course if they're under-age to be using one in any case); taking account of how many friends they bring home or ask to meet up with out of school; keeping an eye on how well they're doing in assessment tests and homework assignments and noticing whether their conversation (whatever there is of it) lacks mention of their usual crowd.

You can help by:

- ▶ dropping a couple of tales of your own experiences of high school friendships into conversation
- ▶ letting your child know that you're always there to listen to their problems if they want to chat
- ▶ getting a friend or relative to chat to them about how things are going for them generally (armed with a few questions about mates to drop in)
- ▶ trying to strengthen links with friends from primary school who haven't joined the same high school
- ▶ encouraging them to join school-led clubs where they might meet other pupils they wouldn't otherwise get to know
- ▶ talking and listening to your child, and letting them know you're there to support them.

Lee was best mates with a gang of boys he'd gone to primary school with, and that continued into high school as they all went up together. But then the others started truanting and wanting Lee to follow suit; thank goodness he didn't think it was worth getting into trouble just to follow the crowd. They started ostracizing him just before the end of the summer term in Year 8 so I took the opportunity of finding out about holiday clubs like tennis coaching and football that he could get involved in at the local sports centre. He found that some of the boys from other forms in his school went to them as well and he went back into Year 9 with at least a few new contacts. It's hard because his other mates are still all together and he hasn't yet found a whole group to hang out with, but I'm so proud of him for doing the right thing, and I think that deep down he's proud of himself too.

Penny, mum to Lee, 14

Insight

Never assume that just because your child doesn't talk to you much they don't want you to talk to them either. It's a fine line to tread between forcing yourself on them when they're genuinely tired or engaged in something else and just leaving them to their own devices. The key thing to remember about pre-teens and teenagers is that they're going through an upheaval in terms of physical and emotional development and may not be able to think as coherently or rationally as they'd like to, so a few timely words of advice, delivered in a low-key way, might just be very welcome.

Spotting low mood or depression in a child

Children, like adults, have mood swings – in fact, as we've already discussed, their mood swings are likely to be more frequent and pronounced than adults', especially as the hormones of puberty kick in. Sometimes, as in adults, genuine depression can occur: the Royal College of Psychiatrists estimates that the illness, although less common in children under 12 years old, affects around five in every 100 teenagers.

The difference between low mood and depression is that low mood is usually transient, whereas in sufferers of depression the problem becomes much worse and gets in the way of normal life. Sometimes there's an obvious reason; in some cases, the reason is there but is less obvious; in other cases there may seem to be no apparent reason for the depression. Whatever the trigger, though, each case must be taken seriously. Genuine depression – which will need to be properly diagnosed – is a medical illness that needs treatment, whether through talking therapies, such as cognitive behaviour therapy (CBT) or medication or a combination of both.

According to Young Minds, a UK charity supporting the mental health and emotional wellbeing of children and young people, signs of depression include:

▶ finding it hard to concentrate, losing interest in school work and play
▶ refusing to go to school, or playing truant
▶ constantly complaining of feeling bored or lonely, even when they have friends
▶ irritability and moodiness beyond the normal range
▶ tearfulness
▶ defiance or violent outbursts
▶ lack of confidence and blaming themselves if things go wrong
▶ disruptive behaviour at school, bullying, stealing or doing other things that lead to them being punished
▶ becoming very withdrawn
▶ self-injury or drinking or taking drugs to excess
▶ sleeping very little or too much.

Younger children may appear to take backward steps in their development, for example with toilet training or eating.

SUPPORTING YOUR CHILD THROUGH LOW MOOD OR DEPRESSION

The first thing to do if you become aware of low mood in your child is to create opportunities to listen (*really* listen) to them and encourage them to talk. It can be hard to strike a balance between probing gently and pressurizing your child into opening up, especially when you're anxious yourself, but any pressure is likely to make them clam up more than ever. You can make subtle changes that will facilitate talking, like turning off the radio or television when you're not actually watching or listening to it; sitting down together in between the different stages of preparing a meal; putting off chores until they're either out or in bed; inviting another adult your child knows and trusts round for supper, then giving them time alone together to chat.

It'll also help if you can ease any pressure on your child, so offer to get a bit more involved with their homework if it's very time-consuming (for example, you could do some basic research); help them with organizing their work; relieve them of household chores so they have more time to focus on school work, and so on. Don't take over, though – that will only take away *necessary* responsibility, making it harder for them to apply themselves when they need to. They might welcome a break from after-school clubs or weekend outings for a while; an easing-off of the pressures of life – however recreational – might be all they need to get back into their stride.

MOOD-BOOSTING FOODS

Eating a healthy, balanced diet contributes to mental wellbeing more than you may imagine. In fact, deficiencies in nutrients including folate, iron, zinc, magnesium, essential fatty acids (EFAs) and B vitamins (especially 12, 6 and 3) can cause low mood and depression. So include plenty of foods rich in these important nutrients.

▶ Good sources of folate include leafy green vegetables, legumes like peas, lentils and beans, bakers' yeast and liver.
▶ Good sources of iron include red meat (especially liver), fortified cereals, soya beans and oatmeal.
▶ Zinc is found in meat, shellfish, milk and dairy foods like cheese, as well as bread and cereal products such as wheatgerm.
▶ For magnesium, eat legumes, nuts, whole grains and vegetables.

- EFAs are found in oily fish, soya beans, flax, hemp seed and green, leafy veg.
- Vitamin B12 is found in meat, salmon, cod, milk, cheese, eggs, yeast extract, and some fortified breakfast cereals.
- Vitamin B6 is found in pork, chicken, turkey, cod, bread, whole cereals (such as oatmeal, wheatgerm and rice), eggs, vegetables, soya beans, peanuts, milk, potatoes and some fortified breakfast cereals.
- Vitamin B3 is found in red meat, poultry, fish and nuts as well as potatoes, pasta and yeast extract.

GETTING TREATMENT

If you feel that your child's low mood is not resolvable at home and suspect they may be depressed, it's important you seek help, either from a school counsellor, pastoral advisor or your GP. There used to be some stigma attached to 'depression' so people were once reluctant to seek help, but it's a very prevalent and much better understood illness today, and it won't resolve without help of some sort. Depending on whether or not you get a referral from your GP for public health treatment, and depending on the length of the waiting list, you may decide to go private, in which case you should ask around for details of an experienced psychologist, therapist or counsellor. Talking therapies can help enormously, especially if there's an underlying problem within the family that would otherwise not have come to light.

Sometimes family therapy might be suggested, where the immediate family is counselled together. This can help children to air any issues they would feel uncomfortable with – or even scared to talk about – at home. In some cases, the problem causing a child's depression may have actually radiated from another member of the family.

Even quite young children can benefit from therapy, although some of their treatment is likely to revolve around role-play, re-enactment, drawing and play as well as talking.

For some children, an early episode of depression is an indicator of a predisposal towards the illness, whereas for others it's a symptom of a one-off, resolvable problem. Take heart: getting depression acknowledged and diagnosed is an important first step towards your child's recovery or management.

It sounded so wrong when Joshua was diagnosed at age 15 with depression and was put on a combination of medication and cognitive behavioural therapy. My wife and I kept wondering if we'd somehow made him ill as we couldn't find any reason why he'd be so unhappy, but the doctors kept telling us there was something chemically wrong in Joshua's brain that could be corrected. We didn't really notice any effect from the treatment until about five weeks in, when Joshua suddenly began to engage with the family more and take an interest in school work and after-school clubs again. It took about two years before he was fully back to his old self, and so far we haven't seen any signs of a relapse. We still don't know what triggered the depression, but we assume it was something to do with going through puberty. Now Joshua's waiting to go to university and I'm fairly confident he'll cope OK although I'm always going to be on the lookout for symptoms whenever he comes home.

Sanjay, dad to Joshua, 18

10 THINGS TO REMEMBER

1 Encourage individuality in your child: children of all ages, but particularly pre-teens and teenagers, tend to have a herd mentality, so praise any positive ways your child chooses to be different from the crowd.

2 If you feel your child is suffering from low mood, think about any recent changes, disruptions or upheavals – however apparently unrelated – they've been through. Talk to them about how they feel things have gone and try to find out if there's a connection.

3 If your child has experienced bereavement and you can't get them to open up, a specialized counselling service such as Cruse Bereavement Care will be able to help. If your child is young, a couple of well-chosen books may explain things in ways they can understand.

4 If you and your partner have separated, reassure your child it's not their fault and that you and your partner will always love them just as much as before.

5 If your child has suffered a crisis of confidence, expect and accept some regression on the way to recovery.

6 Boost your child's sense of self-worth by firing their passion for their interests and giving them a little more responsibility.

7 Build up your child's out-of-school friendships so they aren't reliant on one set of friends in one setting only.

8 Be on the alert for signs of depression in your child and seek help promptly.

9 Don't be stigmatized by the idea of seeking treatment for your child; depression is a serious illness which needs medical intervention.

10 Practise *really* listening by using the reflecting technique, and let your child know you are open to discussion about anything they want to talk about.

7

Confidence as a life skill

In this chapter you will learn:
- *the role confidence plays in different aspects of life*
- *how to build exam confidence*
- *how to help with university applications*
- *how to help with the job search*
- *how to help your child manage personal relationships.*

Confidence for life

Building our children's confidence is like painting the Forth Bridge: it's a job that's never finished. Like working at a marriage, nurturing our kids' egos needs ongoing imagination and commitment. It doesn't always come naturally – and, as in all areas of life, the natural inclination may be to harp on about the bad stuff and just let the good go by without comment or appreciation – but it's a great skill to be able to boost someone's confidence without sounding patronizing or seeming like you're trying too hard.

Remember that, according to some psychologists, for every criticism we receive, we all need to hear five positives in order to maintain self-esteem. That doesn't mean coming over all gushing and over the top every time our kids or partners do something pleasing. A 'positive' could be something as simple as 'Love you' or 'Thanks for being helpful' or 'Good job'; it could be 'You look great today' or 'Well done' or 'Aren't you sweet?'.

Another good tip is to deliver some praise before you criticize: so you could say 'I do appreciate that you've made your bed, but it would be so much better if you could pick your clothes up off the floor, too.' Of course, you're unlikely to manage this every time you need to moan – especially on the occasions when you're really cross and maybe fly off the handle – but even in these cases you can implement some damage limitation by making an appreciative comment as soon appropriate afterwards. It will help you get things 'back to normal', too, instead of you and your child each smouldering with resentment for a prolonged and awkward period.

Try to stay engaged and involved in your child's life – even when they don't seem to want you around or when it would just be more convenient to let them get on with it on their own. The net result will be that they'll more likely to come to you if they're in trouble or having a hard time if they know you're up to speed on their life outside home.

> **Insight**
>
> Ultimately, we need to make ourselves dispensable to our children so that they are equipped to cope with life independently – at least by the time they fly the nest, but preferably by late teenage. It may feel unnatural to be releasing your grip on your child, but the more you allow them to make their own decisions, learn from their mistakes, solve their own problems and exercise their own choices, the more confident they'll be for life.

CONFIDENCE IN SCHOOL...

We've already explored some of the school situations your child may find rewarding or disempowering. Things that will really help to keep their confidence at school, though, include coaching them at home in their weaker subjects (with the school's support); encouraging them to join school clubs and groups so they have a diversity of friendship groups; giving them plenty of opportunities to shine in the subjects they're best at – perhaps by buying a family game that uses the same skills or by setting up some outdoor equipment if they're particularly sporty; keeping in touch with their teachers as far as possible; supporting them at school events like football matches and other performances, and encouraging them to go on school-organized trips.

Part of growing in self-confidence comes from recognizing what you've learned – in terms of life skills as well as formal education – and applying it to other aspects of life. It might help your child to focus on their studies if you point out how, for example, applying themselves to maths will make it easier for them to budget and juggle their own finances later on, or that concentrating in science lessons will teach them a lot about how their body works and how to make the best of their physique, now and in the future.

All of these ideas are applicable to each age and stage of your child's development, although it may not be quite as easy to engage with their teachers once your child's at high school when you'll probably only get an audience between parents' evenings if there is some sort of problem to discuss.

> *Once Lewis had moved on from primary school to high school, it became a bit harder to keep tabs on how well he was doing in different subjects and overall as a member of his form group. The first parents' meeting came late in Year 7 – after Easter – and by then a lot of water had gone under the bridge. We kept in touch with his successes and failures by looking through his exercise books for teachers' comments and test results, and luckily the school was quite receptive to taking phone calls, so whenever we spotted an area we thought needed extra work we contacted the relevant teacher for advice. It worked well and has enabled us to keep Lewis on top of his subjects in a more low-key way. A little bit of home coaching has really helped to build his confidence and he's taken off now in subjects where he was previously struggling a bit.*
>
> Julia, mum to Lewis, 12

... AND AFTER SCHOOL

With your high-school age child, keeping an eye on their friendships and how they are developing without seeming to pry or encroach on their independence is a bit of a balancing act. Your child will gain more confidence if you allow them to make their own arrangements with friends as far as possible, and if you make your home a welcoming place for them while keeping a low profile when they're there, not only will your child have their mates' endorsement that they're cool enough to hang out with, even at home: you'll have the added advantage of knowing where and who your child's with at least some of the time.

It's really important not to act the cool parent though: this will not empower your child or make them feel proud of you – it'll have the opposite effect. Their friends will probably tease them and as a result they'll most likely try to distance themselves from you. Unless it's always been a part of your normal style, you don't need to be wearing the latest fashion, sporting a funky hairstyle or talking in 'teen speak' to gain your child's or their friends' admiration. The whole gang is far more likely to be impressed by an uninvaded space they can take over, some gaming and music facilities and the freedom to raid the fridge (nominated shelves only!) without having to ask you first. When they are a teenager, your child and their mates will really appreciate time alone in the house, too, so lay down some ground rules: let your child know that as long as they respect the rules they'll be allowed the same privilege again, but not otherwise, and leave them to it for a while. Having said that, it might be wise to pop back now and then, especially the first couple of times you entrust the family home to your child's care!

My neighbour has a teenage daughter and is always buying the latest look from the clothes stores aimed at teenagers and twenty-year-olds. At forty-something it makes her look a bit sad, even though she does have the figure for it. It's just that it smacks of trying too hard to be 'down with the kids', and the funny thing is that her daughter has responded by dressing in quite a preppy, conservative way and behaving older than her years in terms of maturity. My own daughter, Dani, who's ten, has already told me she'd absolutely hate it if I was trying to be like her. I think teenagers need to have their own identity, and they'll do whatever it takes to distance themselves from their parents' tastes.

Jan, mum to Dani, ten

Insight

It can be incredibly hard to turn your home over to your teenager and their friends, especially if they haven't always shown it that much respect in the past. However, in most cases, showing teens a degree of trust can result in more mature behaviour. It doesn't always work out, but as long as you make clear that future 'home-alone' time depends on responsible behaviour, your child – if they know what's good for them – will behave accordingly. (It's worth reminding them, too, that the neighbours will also appreciate some respect, so to keep noise levels within acceptable range.)

FROM SCHOOL TO HIGHER EDUCATION OR EMPLOYMENT

If your child wants to go on to higher education, they'll start to narrow the options for their preferred courses and universities in their first year of A levels and make their application at the beginning of Year 13. Your child will get help with the application process from their teachers and from UCAS (the organization responsible for managing UK applications), but it'll help both them and you if you understand the process and get involved.

It can be a bit of a scary time for your child as they start to consider living independently at a distance from friends and family, and they'll probably appreciate your support and input during their investigations. It's certainly worth going to visit universities with them if they'll let you – or at least travelling there with them even if they don't want you to actually go around with them. Either way, you can look around independently and you might even get a different perspective of each place and notice details that your child doesn't. They may, for instance, be focusing more on the social facilities and accommodation than the finer details, and you'll be able to bring these up and discuss them with them afterwards.

Whether your child opts to go to university, take a gap year to go travelling or get a foot straight on the career ladder after they leave school, the self-confidence you've helped build in them will pay dividends. Whatever their next move, they are going to find themselves in a new environment with a whole new set of people, and it'll be important for them to make a good impression as well as get on with their peers or colleagues.

If your child goes to university they'll be sharing accommodation with other people – probably of both sexes – and they'll need to know how to assert themselves as well as how to let others have their say. There will be plenty of compromises to be made – and others who haven't acquired the same skills as your child might naturally look to them to negotiate and help the group come to an agreement, so they'll also need to know how to lead the way and set an example to the others. Don't worry: if you've been following the advice given so far they'll have picked a lot of this up from seeing you and other family members doing the same in your daily life, and by having learned to compromise from when they first started to voice their own opinions and wants.

In the workplace, coming across as self-assured will be even more important – but it's important your child doesn't cross the line into cockiness. Almost every working environment involves some element of competition with colleagues and, however much they like and admire them, your child will probably have to vie with them at some stage for career progression. It sounds aggressive – and it's fair to say it's a different world from when we first launched ourselves on to the job market – but as with other areas of life it's more about knowing how to be assertive (see Chapter 5), which is a skill that everyone can learn, even those individuals who have a tendency towards reticence or shyness.

> *I can't believe the difference in Dan. When he first went off to university he'd been a bit of an over-indulged only child (and much as I was aware that I was cosseting him, I just couldn't help it!). He let me come up and visit him during the second term, and the change was unbelievable. Apparently he'd instigated a system where he and his housemates took it in turns to shop and cook, and where everyone pitched in for essentials like tea, coffee, milk and bread. The others had no idea how to run a household and I suppose that being the only child at home meant we'd interacted a lot together and he'd picked up more than I'd thought. I was expecting him to go to pieces when he had to cope on his own, but he turned out to be the leader of the troops!*
>
> Ella, mum to Dan, 19

IN WIDER RELATIONSHIPS

There will be plenty of relationships to be made once your child has flown the nest. Some will be necessary and others will be out of choice, but a good measure of confidence will help them not only to manage their personal relationships carefully (more of which later) but to avoid being undermined or intimidated by stronger personalities or people in authority. It'll enable them to strike the balance between healthy respect and becoming submissive or aggressive, and will also help them to gain recognition and reward for their efforts.

As in other areas, a lot will depend on what your child has picked up from your interaction with others. If they come from a home where you've had good relationships with neighbours, local shopkeepers and tradespeople, for instance, your child will see this pleasant interaction as the norm and is more likely to replicate it in their dealings with others. It's important they know the difference between healthy co-operation and allowing themselves to be exploited or taken for granted by others.

I've been so proud of the way Adrianna has built some great relationships since going to university, especially as she was always so shy at school. Not only has she got a good, if small, circle of friends, she's also joined some clubs and speaks fondly of the instructors as well as her personal tutor. She seems to have a healthy respect for the lecturers (with the usual exception here and there – but I guess that's to be expected) and the way she's dealt with any problems is amazing. If I'm honest, I was expecting her to be phoning for help all the time, but her friends tend to turn to her for advice now, which is good to know. I hope her listening and practical skills are a result of what she's learned at home over the years.

Dorina, mum to Adrianna, 20

Insight

Remember that even in young adulthood, your child will be looking to you for affirmation and praise. Take opportunities to tell them how proud you are of the way they're maturing, and don't let instances of positive interaction with other people go unnoticed. Mention specific details: you could say, for instance, 'It was thoughtful of you to help that elderly man unpack his trolley in the supermarket, some of those things were awkward for him to lift.'

Building exam confidence from school to university

Your child will be subjected to regular, rigorous testing throughout their school career, and of course this will culminate in GCSEs, AS and A levels. Later, if they go on to university, they'll have a whole new set of exams to cope with, and these will determine to some extent, depending on which course they choose, whether or not they remain on the course and what level of degree they attain. There are ways of building confidence right from the outset, and once you've laid the foundations this should continue into further and higher education. There might be reasons for a loss of confidence along the way though, so here you'll find advice for each stage.

FIRST TESTS IN PRIMARY SCHOOL

Lots of parents – and teachers – have mixed feelings about testing in primary school. From the parents' point of view, it seems like too much stress to put on a young child; from the teachers' point of view it takes up a lot of curriculum time, and the results can either reflect well or badly on their teaching – often largely dependent on the overall calibre of the pupils. Many schools are boycotting SATs (Standard Assessment Tests) and the vast majority of teachers are in favour of replacing them with teacher assessments, where a child's knowledge is assessed by the school rather than outside examiners. Currently SATs are only compulsory at the end of Key Stage 2 in Year 6 (when your child is ten or 11 and about to leave primary education).

Regardless of the future of SATs tests, however, your child won't escape testing altogether and the better prepared they are for it, the better they're likely to cope. The most important thing is to keep the idea of testing low-key, especially when your child is primary school age. The purpose of the tests at this stage is to assess your child's progress and identify any particularly strong or weak areas. The results help teachers to provide for any children who need a bit of extra support as well as those who may be gifted and talented – that is, those with an ability to develop to a level that's significantly higher than expected in their year group.

Things you can do to prepare your child include:

▶ reassuring them that as long as they do their best you'll be very happy, whatever the outcome of the tests
▶ supporting them with going over any work they'd like to refresh their memory about
▶ making sure they have all the equipment they need for tests
▶ ensuring they eat as healthily as possible in the run-up to tests
▶ making sure they get enough sleep
▶ listening to any anxieties they may have, and reassuring them that all will be well
▶ not forcing them to go to school for tests if they're unwell
▶ asking how they feel they did, but not pushing for details on what the questions were, what they wrote, and so on
▶ giving your child plenty of relaxation time between test days
▶ praising your child for any effort made, and for having the maturity to sit their tests without complaint
▶ acknowledging their feelings and telling them it's OK to feel anxious but that they really have nothing to fear
▶ being on hand with lots of cuddles, kisses and reassurance.

Our first child, Jake, got terribly stressed about SATs, and so did we. I expect we passed some of our stress on to him without meaning to. It was a horrible time in the run-up to the tests because his revision wasn't going very well and it just made him panic. He wasn't sleeping well and became very fussy about eating, which just added to the worry. To cap it all, his teacher decided to tell the class that the exam results were a reflection of her teaching ability, and they weren't to 'let her down'! I think it was supposed to be motivating but it was actually the final straw for Jake who became a bit of a nervous wreck. In the end, it really wasn't all that big a deal and luckily he did OK. This time around with Charlie, we've been much more laid back. We figure the tests are of more benefit (or detriment!) to the school than they are of benefit to the kids, so why worry? Jake actually lost confidence throughout the whole spring term, but Charlie is unaffected. I just feel a bit bad for Jake.

Erica, mum to Jake, 13, and Charlie, 11

However non-competitive schools try to make the learning environment, children will nevertheless pick up on where they are ability-wise within their peer group. If your child is less academic than their friends, build them up at home by praising their efforts in home endeavours; talking up their choice of books and films; finding aspects of their personality to praise and reassuring them that there is much more to life than academic brilliance. Find examples among your friends and family of non-academic people your child respects and likes who are perfectly happy and successful in their own right.

If, on the other hand, your child falls into the gifted and talented category, let them dictate how much extra work they want to do to stretch themselves (if they aren't already being sufficiently catered for within the classroom), and talk to your child's teachers about appropriate resources. There are two different but important considerations here: the first is that your child gets the proper support and isn't made to feel inadequate if they don't always live up to their special gifted and talented label; the other is that they don't become a bit too big for their boots and see themselves as superior to other children. In the first instance, reassure your child that it's still OK for them to fail or fall short if they have an 'off day', just as it would be if he wasn't 'gifted and talented'. In the second instance, remind them that their talents are inherent and not something they've worked extra hard to acquire. Finally, treat them as you would if they didn't have any recognized special potential.

If things go wrong

Not all children are able to cope with the stress of tests, no matter how low-key, and some may have an 'off day' or feel generally under par when the tests come round. For this reason, teachers won't use the tests alone to judge a child's ability, and much store is put by class work and homework attainment. If your child is aware that they haven't performed to the best of their ability, or if when their test results come back they're very upset, make as light of it as possible while acknowledging their disappointment. Reassure them that you're not disappointed and that the tests on their own aren't everything. Focus instead of pieces of course work in their exercise books that have got really good comments or those that have earned them house points, stickers or other rewards.

HIGH SCHOOL STUDY STRATEGIES

Really serious study begins in high school – and the more competitive schools will make sure that pupils get into the habit of preparing for and sitting exams very soon after joining, with regular assessments and end-of-year tests. The pressure can be on in those schools that place children in sets: while it's empowering to be moved up a set, to go down can be confidence destroying, and in either event your child will probably prefer to stay in their set because they've made good friends there. Re-setting will usually only result if class work as well as exam work is below or above expected levels, but all the same exams do count towards the final decision.

Children whose strengths lie in more vocational than academic subjects will be expected to master academic subjects like English and Maths up to a certain level whatever future careers they may be planning, and will need five good GCSE passes to be considered for a first-level apprenticeship. There may be more emphasis on course work, but your child will still need your support in their studies as well as in their exams.

Things you can do to help include:

▶ providing them with a quiet area, if possible, where they can spread out and study uninterrupted and without distraction
▶ making sure they have all the materials they need

- ▶ finding out from them what level of input they'd like from you
- ▶ offering to help them organize a study/revision/homework timetable
- ▶ offering to test them when they're ready
- ▶ providing your child with healthy snacks and drinks
- ▶ reminding them to take regular breaks from study
- ▶ encouraging them to get lots of sleep
- ▶ discouraging them from trying to 'cram' late at night the day before a test
- ▶ reassuring your child that you understand they'll do their best
- ▶ giving them lots of praise for effort
- ▶ providing them with some practice papers (ask your school for advice on which) so they can gauge how quickly they'll need to work, and familiarize themselves with the format of the questions
- ▶ encouraging your child to use online revision sites such as *BBC Bitesize*
- ▶ making sure they have plenty of leisure time and relaxation.

If things go wrong

If your child's GCSE grades fall well below expectation, have a chat with their teachers to see what their best options are. Your child may want to do some re-sits and perhaps drop a subject or two, and they might want to reconsider their A level choices. It's important that you support your child and help them to make the best of the situation rather than criticize them for a lack of hard work or commitment when the time for studying and revising has passed. Bite your tongue and help them to focus on future possibilities. If your child is reluctant to talk about what comes next, give them as much time for reflection as possible; reassure them that you'll discuss things with them when they're ready; contact your child's teachers and see if they can put in some time with your child; and don't take any of their bad mood personally.

If it's your child's A levels that have gone wrong it may be that university isn't their next best move after all, and that a vocational qualification might be a better option. If the grades are only a bit below what was expected though, it's worth making a few phone calls to see if they can still have their university place. Encourage them to talk to their course tutors about their options, which may include re-sits or going through the university clearing system. Offer to go with your child to the meetings if they prefer (and accept that they may not).

SUPPORTING STUDY IN HIGHER EDUCATION

By the time your child is studying at university, they should have all the strategies in place that they need for revision. They will also, however, be exposed to even greater peer pressure and all sorts of distractions. If they decide to come home for some of their study time – and if they need to study during university holidays – you can support your child in the same ways as described above for high school learning.

Past papers are an important resource for university students as well as high school pupils. Get your hands on as many as you can and encourage them to time themselves. They probably won't finish in time until they've had lots of practice, so encourage your child to start earlier than they think they'll need to. Past papers aren't just great for self-testing, they're also a fantastic resource for revision as well as teaching things they may not already have learned.

Now, more than ever, your child will need to eat well to increase their brain power and, to some extent, to make up for other lifestyle choices! University students don't tend to be the most rested of individuals: OK, so they may stay in bed most of the day, but they also have a habit of partying hard at night, so any sleep they do get may not be the best quality. Think about sending them some vitamin supplements or takeaway vouchers so they can get themselves something reasonably nutritious to eat. Some restaurant chains sell gift cards, so that's worth considering too, or you could register online with Restaurant Vouchers and send your child a gift card that's valid at all participating restaurants. If there's any chance of you going up to where they are living – and if your child will entertain the idea – how about taking up some home-cooked food for the freezer? Something that's easy to microwave in its container is best. You can buy microwave- and freezer-safe throwaway food savers in supermarkets.

> **Insight**
> It's hard not to interfere once your child has responsibility for their own studies, but it's important you let them organize themselves and put in the hours without you nagging them. It's valuable experience for when they have to become self-motivating in the workplace eventually, so don't keep contacting them to find out if they've been working hard enough.

If things go wrong

It can be a big deal to fail university exams or it can be fairly insignificant, depending on the number of credits attained on the course so far and the number failed. For your child it may feel like a very big deal either way, so be on hand for support. Talk to your child to see if they know what their options are, and encourage them to chat things through with their tutor. If they are in their first year and have failed their exams, it may be that the lost credit points can be made up in their second year, or that they can defer a module or resubmit an assignment, or do re-sits. But it may be that they haven't chosen the best course and should either apply for another within the same university or change course by applying through the clearing system. (Clearing won't necessarily get your child a place on a course in a university they particularly want, though.) Maybe they could consider taking a year out, earning some money and going back to university afterwards.

Your role in all this is, as always, to offer a listening ear and just be there for your child. They might not appreciate any involvement they see as interfering or undermining their judgement, and they might even choose to go off at a complete tangent and do something you consider outlandish instead of pursuing university. This is another situation where it may be best to let him make their own decisions and learn from them. After all, your child has learned to live independently of you while they've been away and will soon have to take full responsibility for their life choices. It's very hard as a parent not to wade in with both feet and try to take charge, but it's not usually the best course of action at this stage, unless your child is showing signs of being unable to cope.

Taking a gap year

Does the prospect of your child spending a year trekking round the world scare you half to death? You're not alone there. It's heart-in-mouth time for many parents when the subject crops up, yet for a young adult it can be an enriching, life-enhancing and eye-opening way to spend a precious bit of time before committing to a life in work. Try not to get too uptight about letting your child go; social networking, smartphones, internet cafés and webcams all provide instantaneous contact if they're in the right place at the right time.

The best way you can support your child and build their confidence for their travels is to show some confidence in their plans yourself. Don't say 'How do you expect to manage halfway round the world when you can't seem to do your own washing or even make a piece of toast at home?'. Do say 'That sounds like a fantastic adventure – and you're bound to come back a much more independent person!'

Gap years that are pre-planned are likely to be the most successful and rewarding, whatever it is your child wants to do – and it may be simply travelling, teaching or volunteering overseas, working abroad or any number of other things. (You'll find lots of advice and ideas online at gapyear.com.) If you're planning to help with finances, you must be magnanimous and not try to impose restrictions. It would be unfair, for example, to say that much as you're willing to pay for an experience *you* consider rewarding, you're not going to donate to an expedition you don't feel is worthwhile. Remember, any experience where you child has had to make their own way and survive on their own mettle will have its own rewards.

Try not to spend the whole time worrying about your child or tracking their whereabouts. This is quite possibly the first experience you'll have had of your child striking out without you and, while it may feel like a baptism of fire (for you both, in fact!), it's also a valuable step in really letting go. Your child will respect you for allowing them their freedom and trusting them to look after themselves and be in touch on their own terms.

It was a sinking moment for me when Nikki announced that she wanted to go travelling for a year. We'd been dreading it, even though we knew it would be a life-changing and valuable experience for her. I think for most parents the worry is that some harm will come to their child when they're on the other side of the world. You feel helpless, and as her dad I've always felt I should be protecting my daughter. Nikki has always been pretty sensible, but not what I'd have called streetwise, so I was actually pleased when she said some of the boys from university were going to meet her and her friend once they reached Rio de Janeiro, about two weeks into the trip. Nikki set up a web page and sent updates home with lots of photos whenever she was able to get to an internet café, so that was reassuring for me and her mum. We also spoke on the phone a couple of times, but it was upsetting to hear her and not be able to see her, so we didn't do it often; the remote internet contact was easier to deal with. We were relieved when she came back early having run out of money. She was all in one piece with no horror stories to tell. We've noticed that she's a lot more her own person now, although I'm a bit ashamed she's seen more of the world than I probably ever will!

Chris, dad to Nikki, 22

Insight

If you need further reassurance that travel is good for your child, remember a gap year looks good on a CV for universities and prospective employers too, as it shows qualities like adventurousness, independence, resourcefulness, confidence (for which, by now, you can claim some of the credit!) as well as an interest in the wider world.

Helping your child find a job

Just as it's not every school or university leaver who knows what they want to do for a career, not all gap-year students come home from their travels with a clear map of the future in their mind. There's such a wide range of choice now that wasn't open to previous generations that it can be mind-boggling and a bit intimidating for young people to try to pin themselves down to one area. Your child may have had work experience as part of their gap year or – depending on when they take it – their A level or degree course and this might have given them some idea of what they do want to pursue, but equally it may only have reinforced what they don't want to do. Don't worry if they seem pretty clueless; there are advantages to this as well as there being pluses to having some idea of possible career opportunities. For example, taking a job that they don't think will particularly grow into a career but will get on the earnings ladder might well lead them in other directions and will at least give your child some networking opportunities, and everyone is more employable when they're in work than when they're not. Of course, if they do know what they want to pursue, you can help your child to look for a way in, even it's only fairly tenuously linked. If they're lucky they'll secure a position doing something related, but even if they can't, starting from an employed position is still going to work in their favour.

The important thing is to have a good CV that stands out from the rest. You can help your child put this together – maybe with the help of a relevant website or job agency – and at the same time start to highlight their strengths and weaknesses and help them think laterally about how their strengths might make them attractive to different industries. Why not sit down and put a comprehensive list together? Don't forget to include any outside interests that show commitment or leadership, either from the past or in the present: having been a prefect at school; being a member of a swimming club; playing in an orchestra or singing in a choir; having taken grade exams for any pursuit; acting with an amateur dramatics group; building up a collection of any sort; trying their hand at rock climbing or pot-holing – it's all worth mentioning and will give a broader idea of your child's personality.

Facing unemployment

There's a real chance that your child will not be able to find employment suited to their qualifications, and the Association of Graduate Recruiters has reported that there's an average of 69 graduates chasing each graduate job. Because of this extra demand, employers have to filter applicants, and the intense competition has meant that 78% are now demanding at least a 2:1 degree. Given that around a third of students graduate with a 2:2, this means that same proportion wouldn't even be considered by most employers offering graduate opportunities.

If your child is finding the job search crushing and hard-going, it's worth having a chat about their options: perhaps they could think about a change of direction and get some on-the-job experience. True, it will mean that their hard work of the past three or four years may feel as if it's been wasted, and they may be very disappointed that they can't get straight into a certain field of work, but realistically they'd be better off trying to get a foot on the ladder – any ladder, in fact – than stewing at home.

Perhaps you have some contacts that would be willing to give your child some work experience or a short-term contract of employment so that their CV will show that they have successfully found work. Maybe they could try voluntary work – at a hospital radio station, helping out at a local youth club or doing some conservation work, for example – that could give them some valuable experience that could eventually lead to employment. It's important they get out of the house and do something rather than languishing at home, losing faith in themselves, feeling bad about asking you for money and becoming disinterested in getting into a work routine. There's more information on volunteering on the government's website www.direct.gov.uk.

Internships are another way of gaining experience in a particular field. They are unpaid posts and may be offered as part of a university course or pursued by graduates after leaving university. Usually lasting several months, they can give a valuable insight into specialized career areas and are a great opportunity for putting theory into practice. You will have to be prepared to support your child financially while they complete their internship, or you could suggest that they combine it with an evening job like bar or restaurant work, or some other out-of-hours role. You can find out more about internships online – there are lots of companies that specialize in this type of work.

If your child really can't get work and finds themselves stuck at home, try not to get on at them all the time to find a job. Help them to devise a weekday timetable so they have a definite getting-up time and a to-do list for each day. Perhaps they could spend the mornings job-hunting and the afternoons doing household chores? Or maybe they can only face the job search once a week, in which case make sure your child is scanning the papers, looking online and registering with likely agencies and head-hunters. Build in some leisure time when they are free to do as they please – otherwise they could end up depressed and demoralized. Encourage your child to keep fit and active by playing sports, cycling, running or swimming – it'll help raise the levels of endorphins ('feel good' hormones) in their system too.

Praise them for any effort made rather than showing too much sympathy and making your child feel they're in a no-hope situation. Thank them for any help they give you in the house; it's a great idea to get them on board with regular jobs so that your child feels they have a purpose. If they really do start to get under your feet and on your nerves, or if they don't seem to be putting much effort into trying to find work, be firm in your encouragement but don't issue any ultimatums you're not prepared to carry through.

Personal relationships

Once your child starts embarking on going out independently, it won't be long before they find themselves interacting socially with both sexes. Up until now they may have treated the opposite sex with a certain amount of bravado or teasing, and will probably have stuck with their own same-sex friends when meeting up out of school. Chances are once they've got their confidence your child will start to take more of a sexual or romantic interest in other people. They may not be sure of their own sexuality and this is a normal part of self-discovery. Plenty of teenagers have encounters with both sexes before their own sexual orientation becomes clear to them. It's quite normal, for instance, for children to have secret crushes on same-sex teachers or other influential adults – and this is a 'safe' way of exploring ambivalent feelings in private.

If your child does discover that they are gay, your reaction (if they choose to tell you) will be crucial to their feelings of self-esteem and acceptance. If you have any prejudices, now would be the time to suppress or, preferably, address them. To reject your child on the grounds of their sexuality could be to lose them altogether. And if they are gay, they will need as much family support as they can get as your child tries to adapt to a life of being perceived as 'different' outside of the gay community.

Whether real or imagined, first crushes and experiences of falling in love are usually extremely intense (even when they're fleeting) and, no matter what you tell your child, they'll probably be unwilling to believe anyone has ever felt this deeply about another person before. (Remember how you felt unique in your experience the first time it happened to you? And how you realized it *wasn't* actually unique the second time you fell for someone?) Be prepared for mood swings, distraction, long periods of reflection, lengthy phone conversations and internet chats, accusations of 'You'd *never* understand!' and more. Don't try to intervene unless you're concerned about the way things seem to be going; even break-ups need to be experienced and handled independently. You can comfort, empathize and soothe, but you can't prevent the pain of broken romance, and nor should you. Most of all, you must take your child's feelings seriously while trying to keep things in perspective for them. Even if you can see what the outcome is likely to be, whatever they're feeling in that moment is absolutely genuine.

All the same, it can be a worrying time to be a parent – not only because you probably won't relish the thought that your child may be embarking on a sexual relationship, but also because you'll have the added worry that any emotional upset will leave your child deeply unhappy. Yes, it's very hard to watch your child in pain – and what parent wouldn't rather take the hurt on themselves? – but your role is to act as a support to your child as they find their feet in more adult relationships. However tempting it may be to try to steer them one way or another, first loves are a kind of rite of passage and will teach your child a lot. Think back to your own early experiences, then imagine how welcome your parents' intervention would have been: probably not very! Your child's confidence will come from knowing that you trust them to conduct and manage their own affairs as far as possible, and that you're there for them when they need you.

When she was 15, Caz told me she was a lesbian and that she was in love with her best friend, Kenzi. I was shocked – and I really believed that by then she'd know her own mind. I tried not to act too upset, but she could see through me and was gutted that I'd taken the news badly. I was imagining what life would be like for her and – perhaps a bit selfishly – how she'd never give me grandchildren. I don't think the two of them had a full-on sexual relationship, although I can't be 100 per cent sure as they were together all that year, but when Caz went to college to do A levels and Kenzi left school to start work, it sort of fizzled out. It was only a couple of months before Caz brought Mark home to meet us, and they've been together ever since. I don't know whether she's actually bisexual or not and she's not up for talking about it any more. I guess time will tell.

Denise, mum to Caz, 17

HOW YOU CAN HELP

There are practical things you can do to help your child enter into personal relationships with confidence.

▶ Provide a comfortable, private space where they feel free to bring friends and partners.

▶ Make sure they're aware of the ground rules regarding sleeping over, bed-sharing and so on. (If you have to remind them in front of a new partner they'll be embarrassed and lose confidence.)

▶ Remind your child that they're a great person to be with – and at the same time take the opportunity to give them a couple of pointers ('I'm sure you don't need reminding, but it's important to put the other person first'; 'How about tidying your clothes away before you bring your friends home?'; 'You don't have to go along with anything you don't want to.'). Your advice may seem to fall on deaf ears, but it'll be registered as long as you don't lecture or nag.

▶ Keep a low profile when your child brings a partner home: don't dominate conversation or try to 'interview' them – and don't embarrass your child by bringing up anecdotes from their childhood, pointing out any habits they may have or saying 'I've heard a lot about you – you're talked about all the time.'

If you suspect your child may be on the brink of a sexual relationship, talk to them privately about whether or not they are both ready for sex, pointing out that physical maturity usually comes way ahead of emotional readiness – for both sexes – but do be prepared to provide contraception along with advice on how and when to use it.

Be there for your child. Don't pry or ask too many probing questions about how a relationship is going – your child has a right to privacy. By now they'll know that they can talk to you if they need to, and it's time for you to take a step back.

10 THINGS TO REMEMBER

1 Although it's easier to criticize than to praise, try to voice pleasure more often than disapproval.

2 Remain engaged with your child's life even when they don't seem to want you involved.

3 Emphasize how skills learned formally in school can be of real practical use in adult life.

4 Don't try to adopt your child's style or be a 'cool' parent; it's important they have their own age-appropriate identity, just as you should!

5 Offer to visit prospective universities with your child – even if you only make the journeys with them and take a back seat for the interviews.

6 Maintain good relationships with your friends, neighbours and anyone else you come into contact with on a day-to-day basis. It'll set a good example to your child.

7 Try not to stress about tests and exams; you'll only reinforce any anxiety your child has of their own.

8 Try not to show too much disappointment if your child doesn't succeed academically; encourage, don't criticize.

9 Provide background support and back-up while your child goes through university and/or takes a gap year.

10 Acknowledge and validate your child's feelings (if they'll share them with you) as they embark on first romantic/sexual relationships.

8

....

Common questions and answers

In this chapter you will learn:
- *how over-parenting can undermine confidence*
- *why shyness doesn't equal a lack of confidence*
- *how goal-setting can improve confidence*
- *whether or not a child can be too confident*
- *how self-esteem affects adult relationships*
- *why confident people are more successful.*

What is 'over-parenting'?

> *My mother has accused me of 'over-parenting' my child. I think she's implying I'm being too protective, but is there such a term as over-parenting, and what does it mean?*
>
> Maggie, mum to Rory, 14

Some parents take protecting their children to the extreme with a tendency to 'over-parent'. This means trying to prevent any disappointments, fulfil every need and want, solve every problem, no matter how small, and generally make the child the centre of their universe. It's a parenting style that, like others, is founded on love and concern, and may well be instinctive in families who have experienced bereavement or tragedy and who have a tendency towards over-protectiveness.

The belief among adults who over-parent is that, in order to be happy, their child must be protected from any of the normal upsets and challenges of daily life; the family unit tends to operate as a whole rather than allowing for individual expression, and the child or children's needs take precedence over the rest of the family's.

There's no doubt that the over-parented child will feel loved and secure; the downside – ironically enough – is that there are dangers that will inevitably arise from this type of upbringing. For starters, when they are a guest in another child's home, the over-parented child won't experience the same levels of over-protection they're used to, so they may feel out of their depth when asked to make decisions, forego expected treats because of a change of plan or generally fend for themselves in the way that their peer group will have been doing for some time as a part of normal development. Then there's the problem that as your child grows older, they may become frustrated with their lack of independence and indulge in risky behaviour whenever they find themselves 'off the leash'.

The over-parented child will probably find it a bigger wrench if and when they come to leave home and start to live independently, and may be the subject of ridicule if they don't have the basic life skills required to live with a group of same-age individuals without parental support. They'll quite possibly lack good judgement about what is and isn't sensible or even acceptable behaviour, having had most things done for them from the earliest time they can remember, and they may have a tendency to over-dramatize small disappointments. Your child may find it difficult to form their own opinions or make choices without someone speaking up for them.

Allowing children to experience disappointment and find solutions to their problems is an important part of parenting. The ability to accept that life is not all plain sailing, to think laterally and to move on without making a crisis out of every situation requires a degree of maturity. It's an important life skill, and to deny it to any child is to deprive them of opportunities to develop resilience, acceptance and pragmatism. And while every good parent wants to protect their child from harm, a certain amount of risk-taking is also part of developing good judgement and learning to be responsible. Of course, as we've seen in earlier chapters of the book, there are ages and stages for introducing small risks and teaching independence. It wouldn't be wise, for instance, to allow a four-year-old to cross a road without holding hands – largely because concentration levels at this age are sporadic; but at age eight or nine, many children can be taught how to behave at crossing lights without having to be restrained physically. This doesn't mean sending them out on their own and keeping your fingers crossed they'll come back in one piece;

it means allowing them to take charge when you're out together: telling you when to start crossing and what you're to look and listen out for as you go. And the toddler who wants to try climbing a new level on the park's equipment could get the go-ahead as long as they agree to you guiding them the first few times they try. It's so much more empowering to encourage this sort of endeavour than to kill any adventurous spirit with alarming warnings that they'll only hurt themselves.

> **Insight**
>
> Being a parent isn't about having children as our own possessions to keep forever; it's about supporting them, nurturing them, allowing them to grow, encouraging their spirit to emerge, letting go, celebrating effort and adventurousness as well as achievement, and rejoicing in the wonderful individual you've brought into the world for others to share.

Does shyness equal lack of confidence?

My eight-year-old daughter is what people might describe as 'painfully shy' when she's in company, but she really shines when she's playing her keyboard or taking a dance class. Is it possible for shy children to be confident?

Harriet, mum to Alice, eight

Yes, it's perfectly possible, although it doesn't go without saying. A child who's shy in the company of new people (which many of us are even in adulthood, although we manage to conceal it), or even with people they know well, may have confidence in other directions. They may, for example, know that they're skilful at playing a musical instrument; they may have a special gift when it comes to dance; or they may have an ability to read fluently that opens up new vistas in their imagination. In other words, shyness only really inhibits social confidence, not the confidence that comes from self-assurance.

Shyness is something that can, with the help of teachers, parents and other involved adults, be outgrown. Sometimes, for example, pairing a shy child with a more confident peer within the classroom can bring the shy child out of their shell; sometimes though, the child is naturally introverted and may prefer to observe rather than take part in group activities. Shyness isn't debilitating in itself, however, and is the natural disposition of many a happy and well-rounded adult.

But the child who lacks confidence within themselves as well as in the company of others – and for whom shyness is crippling in terms of social interaction – might have an anxiety disorder that runs deeper than simply being shy, and which could benefit from counselling or therapy. Talk to your health visitor or GP if you feel that your child might benefit from professional help.

Insight

Try not to label your child. Saying 'Oh well, they're very shy' will reaffirm in their mind that their shyness is a part of who they are and can't be changed. If you feel the need to explain your child's timidity, say 'I think they may be feeling a bit shy today'. This suggests that their shyness is temporary and can be overcome.

How does goal-setting help build confidence?

Every time I try to encourage Callum to try a new sport or hobby, he's always really reluctant. His mum thinks I'm too keen to drop him in the deep end and expect too much too soon. Will setting goals for him improve his confidence?

Tim, dad to Callum, nine

It depends on the child as well as how ambitious the goals are that you set for them. If, for instance, you're coaching your child in football to help improve their skills within the school team, and you set them the goal of getting signed up by a talent scout by the time they are 16, that could be way too much pressure – and it might not be the most realistic goal you could set either. A better, more attainable goal could be to challenge your child to get picked to play for their school team and to have a trial for a local juniors' team outside of school.

It also depends on how well your child is motivated. If they are already a self-starter, setting them goals that are beyond what they have set for themselves may make your child feel inadequate, and this could destroy their confidence, which would be counter-productive. If they find it hard to get motivated, setting them achievable targets with a small reward attached to each might just be the incentive they need. If your child won't read, for instance, you could buy them a popular title among other kids their age and challenge them to get through the first couple of chapters by the end of the week. Offer to read the same book at the same time, and then set up a discussion between the two of you over their favourite meal or at the park. Their self-esteem will benefit, not only from having reached the target, but also from gaining the reward of your time and attention.

> **Insight**
> Reward charts are well known for getting children on side and motivated – and achieving the rewards invariably boosts confidence, so these can work well for any age.

How confident is *too* confident?

> *My daughter often gets the lead roles in school plays and is almost always asked to sing solos in productions and assemblies. I think she might have got a bit big for her boots as a result, and it's making her unpopular with some of her classmates. She's always been very proud of her abilities – as have we – but is it possible for a child to be too confident? I don't want to take the wind out of her sails and destroy her confidence.*
>
> Mary, mum to Aoife, ten

Yes, it's quite possible for a child to become a bit over-confident if positive parenting is taken too far. It's great to praise where praise is due (as we've seen throughout the book), but it's equally important to keep a balance so that your child doesn't become conceited or see themselves as somehow superior to their peers. The sorts of parental behaviour that can lead to children becoming over-confident include:

▶ praising for things a child has had no hand in achieving, like good looks or intelligence
▶ comparing and over-praising a child's achievements with others of lesser ability
▶ talking a child into believing they are the best at everything
▶ allowing them to be too grown-up too soon
▶ having too much of a hand in homework so they appear brighter than perhaps they actually are
▶ being in denial if a child's actual ability level is lower than the parents would like it to be.

The downside of over-confidence in children is that sooner or later they will fail at something – and the fall from the pedestal will be all the harder for them to bear. It may result in public humiliation or, at best, private self-doubt. Over-confidence can also result in a rather arrogant attitude that won't win a child many friends, and can even lead to delusions of grandeur in later life.

It's a tricky business getting the balance of praise right, but if you remember to praise and criticize behaviours rather than the individual; if you support your child at their own natural ability level and encourage realistic aspirations rather than trying to get them to achieve what is beyond them; and if you show your child that humility is all part of respecting other people, you won't go far wrong.

Insight

Withdrawing praise isn't the best way to prevent over-confidence. Continue to praise your child, but make sure that it's constructive, so that you pinpoint exactly what the praise is for. Praise for effort has been found to be more motivational than praise for achievement, as children understand that they can always improve on effort, even if they've reached the pinnacle of their natural ability.

Can lack of confidence impact on adult relationships?

My son has always had something of a downer on himself and is apt to say 'I'm useless' or 'Don't ask me – I don't know anything.' We've tried our best to build him up, but I'm worried his poor self-image will affect his future relationships. Is that likely?

Rosemarie, mum to Damon, 11

It depends on how deep-seated the lack of self-esteem is. Most of us suffer from a drop in self-esteem at different points in our lives: when we experience bereavement or a broken relationship; if we fail at exams; if we go through a period of stress or anxiety or if we lose a job, self-esteem will suffer. But these situations are temporary, and with a bit of work and the determination to pick ourselves up again, self-esteem may be restored.

In people who have suffered from low self-esteem since childhood, however, the implications can be further reaching. Individuals with a poor opinion of themselves may either become 'doormats', allowing themselves to be mistreated by others because they feel they deserve nothing more; or bullies, trying to gain control over others in an attempt to feel superior and thus raise their own feelings of self-worth. Neither is a situation any parent wants for their child. And if your child doesn't adopt either role, chances are there are still aspects of their adult relationships that will suffer: the ability to communicate their wants and wishes effectively; their sex life; asserting themselves in the workplace – all will prove difficult unless they have a good opinion of themselves and their abilities.

Building self-esteem is all about setting small, achievable goals for our children; praising them for any effort as well as achievement, no matter how small; investing our time in them, even if just to play, chat or watch television together; showering them with love and hugs and pointing out their good points without over-praising features over which they have no control, such as good looks or height.

The child whose self-esteem can't be raised despite your best, prolonged efforts, could possibly be suffering bullying outside of the home, so it's worth having a meeting with your child's teachers to find out what's been going on at school, as well as chatting to group leaders of their extra curricular activities. If there's no evidence of bullying, see if the school or any local organizations offer assertiveness training for children. If you still fail to find a reason for your child's low self-worth and there are no courses offered by the school, they might benefit from professional help from a counsellor or therapist. Ask your GP for a referral.

Insight
Plan some regular special time with your child – and mark it on the calendar – to raise their self-esteem. Find something to do together with this time – such as cooking, playing a board game or making improvements to their bedroom – that allows you to work alongside each other. This will make your child feel like an equal partner and give them a real sense of worth.

Why are the most successful people confident people?

I've noticed that the people I know who've had the most success in life are invariably confident types. My daughter, who isn't the most confident girl in the world, is keen to pursue a career as a veterinary surgeon but I know it's going to take a lot of study as well as work experience before she can hope to reach her goal. How can I encourage her to raise her confidence levels and give herself the best chance of success?

Lois, mum to Amy, 17

There are a number of reasons why confident people generally succeed in most areas of life. The first is that they have self-belief: it's a powerful tool for motivation and achievement, as just believing in our own ability to do something can actually raise our potential. So adopting a positive mind-over-matter philosophy could allow us to achieve more than we originally thought possible!

Being assertive means having the ability to put across opinions and desires to other people without being strident or dogmatic. This doesn't always mean that assertive people get what they want all the time, but it does usually mean they're respected for their diplomacy, and will be liked and admired by their peers.

Optimistic people can see their way clear of barriers to their own success, because they've developed the ability to forward plan, think laterally and find solutions to their problems. And because they've set as many things in place for success as possible, they're more likely than most to succeed. For optimists, failure doesn't mean giving up either: they develop the try and try again attitude that means they're likely to get there in the end.

People with a positive self-image tend to focus on their own good points and build on these rather than dwelling on negative points and brooding on what others think of them. When we focus on our negative side, we start to doubt the strength of our own abilities, whereas the more confident among us pour our energy into using our skills to our best advantage.

'Ownership' is a term bandied about more and more frequently these days, and it means taking responsibility for our actions. If we have the ability to acknowledge and 'own' our mistakes and make them good, we can learn from them and move on. But if we're always looking to pass the buck or are in denial that we're responsible for our own mistakes, we can become bogged down in our own failures and feel unable to move forward.

You can teach your child to raise their confidence levels by repeating daily affirmations to themselves. These can be used to reprogram thoughts and actually alter their perception of things, including their own strengths and skills. Your child may feel pretty silly to start with, but if they repeat positive statements like a mantra when they first wake up, and on and off throughout the day, their self-esteem really will improve. Positive affirmations can include: 'I can accomplish anything I set my mind to' or 'I have the ability to make the best of everything' or 'I know I can do it' or 'My friends look to me as a positive role model', and you can encourage them to make up their own too. It's good practice for all the family, come to think of it.

Insight

Successful people aren't afraid to recognize the achievements and successes of others as well as their own, because they're not threatened by other people's abilities. Confidence in your own ability means you're ready to learn from others who might have greater strengths, and to share your own knowledge without feeling threatened.

10 THINGS TO REMEMBER

1 Empty praise and over-protectiveness will undermine your child's confidence. Try to praise selectively and specifically – and let your child learn by trial and error.

2 Allowing your child to try and fail at something is an important part of the learning process, as long as you're supportive and encourage them to try again when they're ready.

3 Labelling your child 'shy' will perpetuate the idea in their head that there's nothing they can do about it.

4 Shy children who shine when they're doing things individually or practising special skills can be just as inwardly confident as outgoing children. Don't fret if your child is shy, as long as they seem happy.

5 Setting small goals to help your child achieve a bigger aim will build their confidence at each stage and encourage them to take the next step.

6 Throwing children in at the deep end with a new hobby or sport won't always pay off; a gung-ho personality might thrive on the challenge, but a less outgoing child could suffer a crisis of confidence.

7 Confident people are popular and successful, but over-confident children are unlikely to make and keep lots of friends. If your child has a special talent, you may need to work at keeping their feet firmly on the ground.

8 A child who is bullied or easily cowed, whether by other children or adults, may become a bully in adulthood. On the other hand, they might just continue to allow themselves to be bullied because that's what they've come to expect. If you suspect your child is being bullied or is a bully themselves, don't delay in talking to the teachers and other adults who care for your child.

9 Your child will learn a lot about adult relationships by observing you. Do your best to be a positive role model whenever you can.

10 Building your child's confidence with specific praise, support and plenty of your time will help them become successful in all their ventures.

Taking it further

EMOTIONAL SUPPORT

Cruse Bereavement Care
Offers support around bereavement.
Website: www.crusebereavementcare.org.uk
Tel: 0844 477 9400

Young Minds
Confidential support for those worried about the emotional problems
or behaviour of a child or young person.
Website: www.youngminds.org.uk
Parents Helpline: 0808 802 5544

Partnership for Children
International charity working to promote mental and emotional
wellbeing in children around the world.
Website: www.partnershipforchildren.org.uk

The British Association for Counselling and Psychotherapy
Holds a register of therapists throughout the UK.
Website: www.bacp.co.uk
Tel: 0870 443 5219

Winston's Wish
Extensive resources aimed at bereaved children and their carers,
including advice on helping children cope with serious illness in
the family.
Website: www.winstonswish.org.uk
Helpline: 08452 03 04 05

ANTI-BULLYING SUPPORT

Bullying UK
UK charity providing information and advice for pupils and parents.
Website: www.bullying.co.uk

Kidscape
The first charity in the UK established specifically to prevent bullying and child sexual abuse.
Website: www.kidscape.org.uk
Helpline: 08451 205 204

NSPCC
Charity dedicated to ending cruelty to children.
Website: www.nspcc.org.uk
Child protection helpline (if you're worried about a child):
0808 800 5000 (or textphone 0800 056 0566)
ChildLine (if you are a worried child): 0800 1111

RELATIONSHIPS SUPPORT

Relate
Offers advice, relationship counselling, sex therapy and support face to face, by phone and through the website.
Website: www.relate.org.uk
Tel: 0300 100 1234

It's Not Your Fault
Practical information for children, young people and parents going through a family break-up.
Website: www.itsnotyourfault.org

STUDY SUPPORT

BBC Bitesize
www.bbc.co.uk/schools/bitesize

Topmarks
www.topmarks.co.uk

FURTHER EDUCATION AND EMPLOYMENT SUPPORT

UCAS
Charitable organization responsible for managing applications to almost all full-time undergraduate degree programmes at UK universities and colleges.
Website: www.ucas.ac.uk/

Association of Graduate Recruiters
An independent, not-for-profit organization dedicated to supporting employers in all aspects of graduate recruitment.
Website: www.agr.org.uk

DirectGov
Government website with information on education, apprenticeships and employment.
Website: www.direct.gov.uk

SUPPORT FOR PARENTS

Family Lives (formerly ParentlinePlus)
Organization run by parents, offering support to parents.
Website: www.parentlineplus.org.uk soon to be www.familylives.org.uk

Netmums
A family of local sites that cover the UK, each one offering information to mothers on everything from where to find playgroups and how to eat healthily to where to meet other mothers.
Website: www.netmums.com

Dad
Offers dads a free and permanent source of the information they're likely to need, from pregnancy, birth and babies to financial, legal and education info – from a dad's perspective.
Website: www.dad.info

BBC Bare Facts
Excellent website for parents, giving approaches for talking with children about sex.
Website: www.bbc.co.uk/barefacts

PRACTICAL SUPPORT

Restaurants Vouchers
Gives access to discounted meals and special offers through restaurants.
Website: www.restaurantsvouchers.com

Index

Image credits

Front cover: © Jose Luis Pelaez Inc/Blend Images/Getty Images

Back cover: © Jakub Semeniuk/iStockphoto.com, © Royalty-Free/Corbis, © agencyby/iStockphoto.com, © Andy Cook/iStockphoto.com, © Christopher Ewing/iStockphoto.com, © zebicho – Fotolia.com, © Geoffrey Holman/iStockphoto.com, © Photodisc/Getty Images, © James C. Pruitt/iStockphoto.com, © Mohamed Saber – Fotolia.com